Sarah Todd first appeared on the Australian food scene in 2014, as one of that season's most popular *MasterChef Australia* contestants. A former high-end fashion model, Sarah epitomises her belief that eating well and looking your best are possible when you use loads of fresh herbs, aromatic spices and beautiful ingredients to create food that is healthy, yet still bursting with flavour. This is her first cookbook.

THE HEALTHY MODEL COOKBOOK

Sarah Todd

Photography by John Laurie

LANTERN

an imprint of
PENGUIN BOOKS

My story

Who'd expect a model with 10 years in the business to have so many delicious recipes to share? For me, they're part of the recipe for a happy life as I am a model that *LOVES* to cook and eat. I'm not talking rice crackers, but food that makes your mouth water. I've travelled the world working for high-end fashion labels modelling on runways and shooting photo spreads for a variety of editorial and advertising campaigns, all the while having a huge passion for food. My creative approach to eating has enabled me to sustain a decade-long career on catwalks and in front of the camera. I've never been one for yo-yo dieting or sticking to unsustainable regimens; instead I have a fresh perspective – not just on eating, but on living. To me, life is about enjoyment and fulfilment, neither of which can be achieved if you're denying yourself the good things. Models aren't meant to eat like this.

I am not a qualified nutritionist; I am simply sharing what works for me. Celebrating food is one of life's great joys, and here I show you how to eat nutritious food without losing that delicious sense of indulgence. It's all in the art of balance – smart, fresh cooking blended with a healthy attitude to life. Embrace the chance to break with energy-sapping habits and build an approach to food that is so enjoyable it will sustain you for a lifetime. Great food doesn't need to be flavourless!

My aim is to make wholesome eating achievable, affordable, simple and, above all, delicious.

My five food 'rules':

1 It is possible to eat well and not feel like you are missing out.

2 I aim to eat consistently to maintain my weight and maximise vitality, so I have more energy to be active.

3 Always cook with a balanced range of local, fresh seasonal produce. I champion real food, which means whole, organic, nutritious, delicious homemade. This includes buying grass-fed meat and organic fruit and vegetables. (You can start this slowly by choosing vegetables that grow above ground as these are likely to have more insecticides.)

4 No kilojoule counting or exclusion of key food groups. While I minimise high-starch foods, gluten and refined sugar, I cook with butter and ghee and don't take the skin off my chicken!

5 Absolutely no extreme diets – they are impossible to maintain.

By adhering to these key principles, I feel more energised, sleep better and don't feel bloated or as though I need to lie down and have a nap after lunch.

Finding balance

I intend the recipes in the Breakfast, Soups, Salads and Mains chapters of this book to be complete meals in their own right. When I think about creating a dish, the main points I consider are how to balance it and whether I am consuming enough nutrients to give me the energy I require throughout the day.

I love cooking, but I also love not having to cook from scratch every day! Cooking in batches allows you to have a bank of wholesome meals at the ready. Cooking with leftovers also makes you think creatively about the ingredients you use.

Finding this balance has been quite a journey for me. After suffering at various times from polycystic ovarian syndrome, acne, tiredness and iron deficiency, I tried eliminating certain ingredients and gave extreme diets a go. Eventually I found a naturopath and started on this path of believing that my overall wellbeing largely comes down to the food I eat.

My basic rule of thumb is to use fresh produce and aim for a balance of 40 per cent protein, 40 per cent carbohydrates and 20 per cent fat in every meal. Of course, I don't always stick to this, however; it's a great guideline and over time I've found it absolutely stops all my cravings. From there, I add loads of flavourings, such

as spice mixes (see pages 186–193). If I'm ever still hungry, I fill up on vegies, such as any of the vegetarian salads in the salads chapter (see pages 52–87) rather than protein or fats. I have a hectic schedule and need to nourish myself so I don't feel hungry or tired – I created the recipes in this book to achieve this. Eating a healthy snack can prevent overeating at mealtimes, so rather than pushing through those hunger pains, try some of my favourites on pages 88–95.

Spices and herbs are the ultimate way to take a dish to the next level in a healthy way, so I've included lots of recipes for spice mixes, dressings and condiments on pages 186–193 to give whatever you are cooking a big flavour boost.

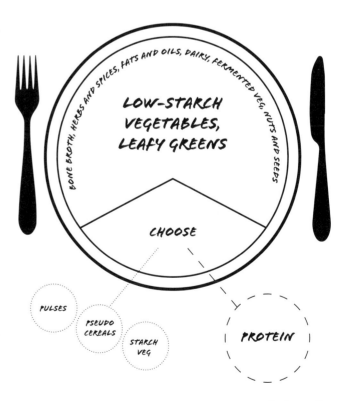

LOW-STARCH VEGETABLES, LEAFY GREENS

BONE BROTH, HERBS AND SPICES, FATS AND OILS, DAIRY, FERMENTED VEG, NUTS AND SEEDS

CHOOSE

PULSES

PSEUDO CEREALS

STARCH VEG

PROTEIN

An everyday day

For me, a good night's sleep combined with relaxation and positive thoughts during the day are essential. Sleep is free, it's easy, it feels amazing, and nothing else resets you in quite the same way.

During my early years I suffered from chronic migraines. I'm very pleased to say I haven't suffered one since I started living a more balanced life. Along with eating fresh, wholesome foods, this means taking a moment for myself every morning to calm and focus my thoughts in the present and be thankful for what I have right now.

Taking the time to nourish your mind and body is the most important thing you can do for yourself and others. Understanding the impact that the mind and the body have on one another and nurturing that connection is really important.

We live in a digital world, saturated with information and over-stimulation. If we're not reading emails on our laptops, we're Instagramming, posting on social media or being distracted by another digital medium. Meditating is an opportunity to dump any stress from the day, create clarity and calm the mind.

Starting the day with a good breakfast is an essential part of my health equation. Eating a nourishing breakfast kickstarts your digestion and metabolism, so you can function at an optimal level throughout the day. I'm not one for skipping meals, as it signals to the brain that the body is 'starving', which can trigger the release of stress hormones (such as cortisol), creating all kinds of hormonal and digestive havoc!

As a guide to the way I like to structure my meals each day, I eat quite a lot every day and my biggest tip is to spread it out. There is more pleasure in having five smaller meals a day than trying to hold out for three larger ones – this seems to keep my metabolism on track, too.

AN ORGANISED

PLAIN NOTEBOOK

My daily routines

• I follow the **AYURVEDIC PRACTICE** of scraping my tongue with a tongue scraper for fresh breath and improved oral health upon waking.

• I kickstart my metabolism with a glass of **HOT WATER AND LEMON.**

• This is followed by a **NUTRITIOUS BREAKFAST** (see pages 14–31).

• I aim to eat **5 MEALS A DAY**, including snacks, so I eat regularly and do not skip meals.

• I am conscious of what I drink and generally have a **GREEN TEA** and glass of **LEMON WATER,** plus 2–3 litres of water each day.

• My **COFFEE OF CHOICE** is a piccolo, however, I don't always have this first thing in the morning. I often wait until right before my workout, either later in the morning or just after lunch, to savour that buzz from a coffee and get a little extra energy.

• Whenever my schedule allows, **I PREPARE MEALS AND SNACKS THE NIGHT BEFORE**, so I know I always have something healthy and homemade to eat.

• While I do not count kilojoules or weigh portions, I keep an eye on **PORTION SIZES.** I've created a basic chart to give you an indication of portion size for protein (see page 3).

• For me, the excitement of **PLANNING YOUR MEALS** each day adds to the fun; I believe it's an integral part of the cooking process. I like to think about the weather: do I feel like a cosy dish or something fresh and summery? Do I feel like chicken or lamb? Making this process enjoyable keeps it fresh and stops me getting bored.

• If you are anything like me and have a massive **SWEET TOOTH**, you need the option of dessert. I think it's much better to embrace and fulfil the craving (within reason) than ignore it. I have created a bunch of delicious desserts (see pages 156–175) that will curb your cravings without going overboard.

• I believe it is vital to **GET OUTSIDE EVERY DAY** for fresh air, a sense of vitality and an all-important dose of vitamin D. Daylight also helps to reset your internal body clock – also known as the circadian rhythm – leading to better sleep and allowing your body to tune into what it needs.

• Stay **ACTIVE.**

Three tips for being healthier at work

1 Take a packed lunch. I recommend making extra portions of dinner and freezing or refrigerating them so you have a supply of nutritious food to eat on-the-go. Invest in a thermos and bring in hot comforting and nourishing soups and stews. Salads are also great. You'll save money, too!

2 Drink lots of water and stay hydrated. Air conditioning, heating, sugary drinks and coffee do not support our immune system, skin or brain. Try flavouring water with lemon, orange, cucumber slices and fresh mint to add interest. Try one of the pep-me-up teas on pages 153 to 154 as a great mid-morning or afternoon boost in place of coffee or a trip to the vending machine. A punchy blend of ginger, turmeric, cayenne and lemon is energising and immune boosting and won't be followed by an energy crash.

3 Take a break from your desk and get some fresh air. It's easy to sit and stare at a screen all day, but better to keep moving as our bodies are designed to. It's not healthy to be constantly 'on' and communicating every moment of every day. Clear some time to get out in the fresh air and you'll be more productive. Finding the time to meditate (morning or night) will also help to clear the mind – decision-making will become easier and creativity will flow.

This book is not about dieting; it's about choosing to embrace a sustainable lifestyle that creates an abundance of energy and positive thoughts. In turn, this will give you the willpower to workout for an extra five minutes and take the stairs instead of the lift, as well as clarity and calmness so you can live a happy, healthy life.

I've enjoyed creating a cookbook that can be used every single day to cook fresh, satisfying meals, from nourishing breakfasts and easy weeknight dinners to revamped comfort foods and more elaborate dishes for dinner parties.

Breakfasts

Simply put, we are breaking the fast after a night's sleep. Prolonging your body's starvation mode by regularly skipping breakfast will lead to a slower metabolism.

Many of us have slipped into the habit of having a coffee for breakfast, a light lunch and a heavy dinner; this just doesn't make sense to me. I love the saying, 'Breakfast like a king, lunch like a prince and dine like a pauper.' Breakfast sets the tone for the rest of my day. My body has longer to digest a high-kilojoule breakfast, leaving me satisfied for longer. With such a hectic schedule, fueling my body with enough energy to last the day is a necessity.

I've shifted the focus and concentrated on breakfast as my main meal. While this means taking more time in the morning, the trade-off is I can take it a little easier in the evening with quick weeknight meals that give me more time to relax.

Breakfast granola with honey yoghurt

MAKES ABOUT 7 CUPS (850 G) • 10 MINUTES PREPARATION + COOLING TIME + 4–5 HOURS DRAINING • 50 MINUTES COOKING

Paired with creamy honeyed yoghurt, this crunchy wholegrain granola looks and tastes like a total winner, yet is effortless to make. Ensure you have a large airtight container to store it in and it'll stay fresh for a couple of weeks. Keep the nutmeg to a bare minimum – it has a strong flavour, so a little goes a long way. If you're not up to making the saffron yoghurt, just serve it with your favourite bought Greek-style yoghurt instead.

180 g coconut oil (see page 194)

$^1/_4$ cup (60 ml) pure maple syrup

1 teaspoon vanilla bean paste

2 cups (180 g) rolled oats

3 cups (105 g) puffed rice (see page 195)

$^1/_2$ cup (80 g) pepitas (pumpkin seed kernels)

$^1/_2$ cup (75 g) sunflower seeds

1 cup (160 g) almonds, coarsely chopped

2 teaspoons ground cinnamon

$^1/_4$ cup (35 g) unsalted shelled pistachios

$^1/_2$ cup (25 g) shaved or flaked coconut

diced mango, sliced peach or nectarine, shaved coconut and finely grated orange and lemon zest, to serve

milk (optional), to serve

HONEY YOGHURT

1 cup (280 g) Homemade Yoghurt (see page 18) or natural Greek-style yoghurt

2 tablespoons milk

pinch of saffron threads (optional)

$^1/_4$ cup (90 g) honey

pinch of ground nutmeg

For the saffron yoghurt, wrap the yoghurt in muslin, then hang over a bowl in the fridge for 4–5 hours to drain and thicken.

Preheat the oven to 150°C (130°C fan-forced).

Melt the coconut oil in a small heavy-based saucepan over low heat, add the maple syrup and vanilla paste and stir, then set aside.

Combine the oats, rice, seeds, almonds and cinnamon in a large bowl, then pour the maple syrup mixture over and stir to coat evenly. Spread over a baking tray lined with baking paper. Bake, stirring occasionally, for 40–45 minutes or until golden and evenly toasted.

While still warm, press flat with a palette knife (this helps to form clusters) and leave to cool on the tray.

Meanwhile, for the saffron yoghurt, place the milk in a small heavy-based saucepan and warm to just below a simmer. Add the saffron, give it a quick stir, then leave to cool for 5 minutes.

Put the yoghurt into a bowl, then add the honey and use a wooden spoon to beat well for 5 minutes or until well blended and smooth; it should have a creamy consistency. Add the saffron milk, along with the nutmeg. Mix well, cover with plastic film and chill for at least 1 hour. (Makes about 1 cup [280 g]. Leftovers can be stored in the fridge for up to 1 week.)

Coarsely crumble the granola into clusters, then combine in a bowl with the pistachios and coconut. Store in an airtight container until required. Leftover granola will keep for 2 weeks in the pantry.

Serve the granola topped with the fruit, coconut and citrus zest, and the yoghurt in a bowl alongside.

Vanilla tapioca porridge

For me, nothing is more synonymous with winter than a warm bowl of porridge. My delicious tapioca alternative can be served hot or cold, so you can enjoy the sensation of tapioca pearls popping in your mouth all year round. Light and refreshing with summer berries or warm and comforting with winter fruits, you just can't go wrong.

1 cup (200 g) tapioca pearls
2 cups (500 ml) water, or enough
    to cover
1 cup (250 ml) milk
1 cup (250 ml) coconut milk
2 tablespoons honey
1 teaspoon vanilla bean paste
berries, pure maple syrup, shaved coconut,
    micro-herbs, edible flowers
    and hazelnuts, to serve

Place the tapioca and water in a bowl and leave to soak overnight.

Combine the milk, coconut milk, honey and vanilla in a heavy-based saucepan, then bring just to the simmer over medium heat, stirring to combine.

Drain the tapioca and add to the milk mixture, then stir continuously over medium heat for 4–5 minutes or until the mixture has thickened and the tapioca is tender and translucent. Remove from the heat and divide among 4 bowls.

Drizzle a little maple syrup over the berries, then place on top of the porridge and scatter with coconut, micro-herbs, edible flowers and hazelnuts. Serve immediately.

The perfect omelette with rocket, parmesan and pear salad

My perfect omelette is flavour-packed and never gets boring. This version, with loads of greens and delicate, delicious flavours ticks all the boxes. The crunch of pecans and the parmesan in the salad are the icing on the cake.

ghee (see page 194), for cooking

$^1/_2$ onion, finely chopped

1 small zucchini (courgette), coarsely grated

1 cup (large handful) baby spinach leaves

4 eggs

sea salt and freshly ground black pepper

$^1/_4$ cup (20 g) finely grated parmesan

ROCKET, PARMESAN AND PEAR SALAD

$^1/_2$ cup (handful) rocket

$^1/_4$ cup (30 g) pecans, toasted and chopped

50 g parmesan, thinly shaved

$^1/_2$ pear, thinly sliced

extra virgin olive oil, for drizzling

sea salt and freshly ground black pepper

balsamic glaze or balsamic vinegar,
    for drizzling

Heat 1 tablespoon ghee in a small heavy-based saucepan over medium heat. Add the onion and cook for 10 minutes or until soft and translucent; you don't want to get any colour on the onion, so add a drop of water to the pan to stop it browning, if necessary. Add the zucchini and cook for 2 minutes. Add the spinach, then remove from the heat and set aside.

Break the eggs into a large bowl and whisk gently. Add the vegetable mixture and mix until well combined. Season with salt and pepper.

Heat a large heavy-based frying pan over medium heat, then add 1 teaspoon ghee. When hot, add the egg mixture, spooning it over the pan and making sure that the mixture evenly covers the surface. Reduce the heat to low and cook for 5 minutes or until just before the top is cooked. Scatter the parmesan across the omelette, then fold it in half.

For the salad, put the rocket, pecans, parmesan and pear into a large bowl and mix. Drizzle with olive oil and season with salt and pepper.

To serve, place the omelette on a plate and add the salad on top. Drizzle balsamic glaze or vinegar over the salad.

Bircher muesli

I tasted my first bircher muesli during a stay on Hayman Island and I was hooked. Healthy, delicious and no cooking required.

180 g (2 cups) rolled oats

2 cups (500 ml) coconut water

2 tart green apples, such as Granny Smith

1 cup (250 ml) coconut milk

$^1/_4$ cup (90 g) honey

125 g blueberries

roasted hazelnuts, skinned and
    crushed, to serve

The night before, mix the oats and coconut water in a bowl. Cover and soak overnight in the fridge.

In the morning, grate the apples, with their skin on, and add to the bowl of oats. Add the coconut milk and honey and mix together well. Divide the muesli among 4 bowls, top with the blueberries and hazelnuts, then serve.

Zucchini and pea pakhoras with smoked salmon and paprika yoghurt

MAKES 18 • 15 MINUTES PREPARATION + 30 MINUTES DRAINING • 35 MINUTES COOKING

A slight twist on an onion pakhora takes this dish in a new direction. The subtle flavour of zucchini with the sweetness of pea is mixed with the chickpea flour and spices, then beautifully balanced by the salmon and yoghurt. This dish makes a decadent breakfast and also works well for lunch.

1¹/₂ zucchinis (courgettes)

2 teaspoons sea salt

1 onion, finely chopped

1 teaspoon ground cumin

1 teaspoon ground coriander

1 teaspoon Garam Masala (see page 188)

¹/₂ cup (60 g) frozen peas

1¹/₂ cups (225 g) chickpea flour

1 cup (250 ml) water, approximately

vegetable oil, for shallow-frying

100 g smoked salmon

salmon roe, baby cress and lemon
   wedges, to serve

PAPRIKA YOGHURT

100 g Homemade Yoghurt (see page 181)
   or natural Greek-style yoghurt

1 teaspoon smoked paprika

Grate the zucchinis into a bowl, then coat with the salt and leave to stand for 30 minutes; this will extract the liquid from the zucchini. Squeeze the excess liquid from the zucchini into the sink and pat dry with paper towel. Transfer to a clean bowl.

Add the onion, spices and peas to the zucchini and stir. Add the chickpea flour, bit by bit, mixing continuously to coat all the ingredients. Add the water, bit by bit, stirring until you have a thick batter-like consistency; you may not need it all.

Pour a 2 cm layer of vegetable oil into a heavy-based frying pan, then heat over medium heat. Working in batches, add large tablespoons of the batter mixture to the pan, pressing it slightly to flatten. Pan-fry for 2 minutes or until golden underneath, then turn over and cook for another 2 minutes. Remove from the pan and drain on paper towel. Repeat with the remaining batter. (Makes about 18.)

For the paprika yoghurt, place the yoghurt in a small bowl, then stir through the paprika.

Serve the pakhoras with the paprika yoghurt, smoked salmon, salmon roe, baby cress and lemon wedges.

Quinoa nasi goreng

SERVES 4 • 15 MINUTES PREPARATION + OVERNIGHT SOAKING • 25 MINUTES COOKING

Now I know this is a bit of an out-there dish for breakfast, however, I strongly believe in fuelling ayour body for the day ahead and this dish does just that. Nasi goreng is a delicious alternative to the traditional heavy English bacon and egg breakfast. If you can't bring yourself to eat this for breakfast, go ahead and have it for lunch or dinner. It's sure to impress.

1 cup (190 g) quinoa (see page 195), soaked overnight in cold water

ghee (see page 194), for cooking

2 chicken thigh fillets, fat trimmed, cut into 2 cm pieces

175 g bacon, rind and fat removed, cut into 1 cm dice

1 onion, thinly sliced

2 cloves garlic, thinly sliced

1 carrot, finely diced

1 stick celery, finely diced

200 g small peeled cooked prawns

200 g Chinese cabbage (wombok), finely shredded

80 g bean sprouts

2 tablespoons kecap manis

1 tablespoon soy sauce

4 eggs

2 tablespoons crisp-fried shallots (available from Asian food stores), to serve

Drain the quinoa, then cook in a large heavy-based saucepan of boiling water following the instructions on the packet until tender.

Meanwhile, heat a large wok over medium heat. Add a teaspoon of ghee and heat until just smoking. Add the chicken and stir-fry for 3 minutes or until brown and just cooked through. Transfer to a bowl. Add the bacon to the wok and stir-fry for 2 minutes or until brown and crisp. Transfer to the bowl of chicken.

Leaving the juices in the wok, add the onion, garlic and a dash of water, stirring to lift the flavour off the bottom of the wok and stop the onion from browning, then cook for 2 minutes or until the onion is soft. Add the carrot and celery and stir-fry for 3 minutes or until the carrot is tender. Add the prawns and stir-fry for 2 minutes or until heated through.

Return the chicken and bacon to the wok and add the cabbage, then stir-fry for 3 minutes or until the cabbage has wilted. Add the drained quinoa, bean sprouts, kecap manis and soy sauce, then stir-fry for 2 minutes or until heated through. Transfer to a large bowl. Cover with foil to keep warm.

Heat a large non-stick frying pan over medium–high heat with a teaspoon of ghee. Crack the eggs into the pan and cook for 2 minutes or until the whites are set and the yolks are almost set (for a soft yolk) or until cooked to your liking.

To serve, spoon the nasi goreng into 4 bowls. Top each with a fried egg and sprinkle over the fried shallots. Serve immediately.

Scrambled eggs with spicy cavolo nero

SERVES 2 • 5 MINUTES PREPARATION • 12 MINUTES COOKING

Wrap this in your favourite tortilla or flatbread for a fantastic breakfast on the go.

ghee (see page 194), for cooking
1 teaspoon Garlic Paste (see page 180)
$\frac{1}{2}$ small fresh red chilli, finely chopped
100 g cavolo nero, shredded
2 spring onions, thinly sliced
sea salt and freshly ground black pepper
4 eggs
**toasted Flax Bread (see page 178) and
    flat-leaf parsley leaves, to serve**

Heat a teaspoon of ghee in a large heavy-based frying pan over medium heat. Add the garlic and saute for 2–3 minutes or until golden. Add the chilli and saute for another 1 minute, then add the cavolo nero and spring onion and cook for 3–4 minutes, until wilted. Season to taste and set aside.

Meanwhile, crack the eggs into a bowl and whisk to combine, then season to taste. Heat a teaspoon of ghee in a heavy-based frying pan over low–medium heat, then add the egg and stir with a spatula to ensure it doesn't stick to the base of the pan. Cook for 3–4 minutes or the egg is almost set.

To serve, spoon the scrambled eggs onto the toast and serve topped with the cavolo nero mixture, parsley and a grinding of pepper.

Smashed avocado and feta on toasted flax bread

SERVES 4
5 MINUTES PREPARATION

I could eat this any time of the day and, with the addition of umami in the form of a hidden spread of Vegemite, it will put a 'rose in every cheek' (see picture opposite).

1 avocado, halved, seeded, peeled
lemon juice, to taste
30 g feta, crumbled
8 slices Flax Bread (see page 178), toasted
Vegemite, to taste
sea salt and freshly ground black pepper
Dukkah (see page 190), for sprinkling
herbs, such as coriander cress or lemon
    balm leaves (optional), to serve

Mash the avocado to a fine paste, add a squeeze of lemon to prevent discolouring, then finish by stirring in the crumbled feta.

Spread the toast with Vegemite, then top evenly with avocado and feta mixture and season with salt and pepper. Sprinkle with dukkah and scatter the herbs over, if using, then serve.

Braised leek and peas with a poached egg

SERVES 4
10 MINUTES PREPARATION
10 MINUTES COOKING

I love to throw in some greens to make a nutritious breakfast. Combined with salty pancetta, sweet leeks and a poached egg, you have the perfect start to the day.

ghee (see page 194), for cooking
1 leek, white part only, cut into
    1 cm-thick rounds
50 g pancetta, roughly chopped
1 stick celery, finely chopped
$\frac{1}{2}$ carrot, finely chopped
400 g frozen peas
50 ml white vinegar
4 eggs
snowpea (mange-tout) shoots, to serve
sea salt and freshly ground black pepper

Heat a heavy-based frying pan over medium–high heat, then add a drizzle of ghee. Add the leek rounds to the pan, placing them flat in a single layer, then cook for 2 minutes to char slightly, flip and repeat on the other side. Add the pancetta and cook for 1–2 minutes, until slightly crispy. Add the celery and carrot and toss for 1 minute, then add the peas and enough water to just cover. Cook for 4 minutes or until the liquid is almost completely reduced and the peas are tender.

Meanwhile, add the vinegar to a large heavy-based saucepan of simmering water, then add the eggs and cook over medium heat for 2½ minutes for soft-poached. Drain on paper towel.

Divide the braised vegetables among 4 plates, then top with a poached egg, scatter with snowpea shoots, season with salt and pepper and serve.

Field mushroom frittata

Sometimes eating well really can be this simple. I like to use whatever mushrooms are in season for this satisfying frittata. In autumn I would use pine mushrooms, but I love to mix it up with different textures and flavours of mushrooms, so I can still enjoy this year-round.

ghee (see page 194), for cooking

200 g field or other mushrooms, cut into
   5 mm-thick slices

sea salt and freshly ground black pepper

8 spring onions, including green parts,
   cut into 1 cm lengths

1 clove garlic, finely chopped

2 sprigs thyme

8 eggs, lightly beaten

$^1/_2$ cup (40 g) freshly grated parmesan,
   plus extra to serve

Preheat the oven to 180°C (160° fan-forced).

Heat a heavy-based 22 cm frying pan over high heat (mine is cast iron). Add the ghee and saute the mushrooms until softened, then season with salt and pepper and transfer to a bowl. Add the spring onion and garlic to the pan and saute until fragrant. Return the mushrooms to the pan, add the thyme and stir well.

Pour the egg over the vegetables and stir briefly for 1 minute or until it starts to set on the base of the pan. Sprinkle the parmesan over the frittata. Transfer to the oven and bake for 10–15 minutes or until golden and set.

Remove from the pan, cut into wedges and serve with extra parmesan.

Smoked beans on toast with bocconcini

SERVES 4 • 20 MINUTES PREPARATION + OVERNIGHT SOAKING • 1 HOUR COOKING

A little upgrade on the classic beans on toast brekky, this one packs a punch but mainly in the flavour area, as it is spicy without being hot.

150 g dried kidney beans, soaked overnight in cold water

150 g dried borlotti beans, soaked overnight in cold water

2 teaspoons ghee (see page 194)

1 onion, finely diced

$1/_2$ carrot, finely diced

1 stick celery, finely diced

2 rashers smoked bacon, finely diced

1 tablespoon pure maple syrup

2 tablespoons smoked paprika

1 teaspoon ground chilli

1 teaspoon ground cumin

1 fresh bay leaf

3 cups (750 ml) Chicken Broth (see page 33) or water

toasted Flax Bread (see page 178)

torn bocconcini and baby cress, to serve

Drain the beans and rinse thoroughly.

Heat the ghee in a heavy-based saucepan over medium heat. Add the onion, carrot and celery and cook for 10 minutes or until soft. Add the bacon and cook for 2 minutes. Add the beans, maple syrup, spices and bay leaf, then cover with the chicken broth or water. Bring to the boil, then reduce the heat to low and simmer for 45 minutes or until the beans are tender and the liquid has reduced to a thick sauce consistency.

To serve, spoon the beans onto your toasted flax bread, top with bocconcini and baby cress.

Broths

Dem bones, dem bones, dem broth bones . . .

Nutrient-rich homemade broths add a depth of flavour that can't be found on a supermarket shelf. There is good reason we offer chicken soup to loved ones struck down by the dreaded cold – the bone broth in that soup contains collagen/gelatine, glucosamine, calcium, magnesium and amino acids. My broth recipes are extremely simple and inexpensive (ask your local butcher for the bones). I like to use these as a base for all my soups, and use the chicken broth even for those that are vegetable based.

Beef broth

MAKES ABOUT 3-4 LITRES
5 MINUTES PREPARATION
8-12 HOURS COOKING

---

2 kg beef bones, cut into 2 cm pieces
(ask your butcher to chop them)
2 tablespoons apple cider vinegar
(see page 194) or lemon juice
1 onion, unpeeled, halved
1 carrot, cut into 3 pieces
2 sticks celery, cut into 3 pieces
2 sprigs thyme
1 teaspoon white peppercorns
2 fresh or dried bay leaves

Place all the ingredients in a large stainless-steel stockpot and cover with cold water, as slow heating helps bring out the flavours. The water should cover the bones by approximately 5 cm, still leaving a little room at the top of the pan. Cover with the lid and bring to the boil. Reduce the heat to low and simmer for a minimum of 12 and maximum of 24 hours. (I prefer a low and slow cook time to extract all the nutrients from the bones.)

Occasionally skim off any fat or foam that rises to the surface and top up with additional water as needed to keep the ingredients covered. Strain the broth through a fine-mesh sieve into a bowl and discard the solids.

Once the broth has cooled, fat will rise to the surface. When this hardens, you can discard it.

The stock will keep for 5 days in the refrigerator or may be frozen in an airtight container for up to 6 months. (I like to freeze it in silicone ice cube trays, so it is easy to add a burst of flavour to whatever I'm cooking.)

Chicken broth

MAKES ABOUT 3-4 LITRES
5 MINUTES PREPARATION
6-12 HOURS COOKING

---

2 kg chicken carcasses, chopped into 2 cm pieces
(ask your butcher to chop them)
2 tablespoons apple cider vinegar
(see page 194) or lemon juice
1 onion, unpeeled, halved
1 carrot, cut into 3 pieces
2 sticks celery, cut into 3 pieces
2 sprigs thyme
1 teaspoon white peppercorns
2 fresh or dried bay leaves

Place all the ingredients in a large stainless-steel stockpot and cover with cold water, as slow heating helps bring out the flavours. The water should cover the bones by approximately 5 cm, still leaving a little room at the top of the pan. Cover with the lid and bring to the boil. Reduce the heat to low and simmer for a minimum of 6 and maximum of 12 hours. (I prefer a low and slow cook time to extract the nutrients from the bones.)

Occasionally skim off any fat or foam that rises to the surface and top up with additional water as needed to keep the ingredients covered. Strain the broth through a fine-mesh sieve into a bowl and discard the solids.

Once the broth has cooled, the fat will rise to the surface. When this hardens, you can discard it.

The stock will keep for 5 days in the refrigerator or may be frozen in an airtight container for up to 6 months. (I like to freeze it in silicone ice cube trays, so it is easy to add a burst of flavour to whatever I'm cooking.)

Lamb broth

MAKES ABOUT 3–4 LITRES
5 MINUTES PREPARATION
8–12 HOURS COOKING

---

2 kg lamb bones, chopped into 2 cm pieces
(ask your butcher to chop them)
2 tablespoons apple cider vinegar
(see page 194) or lemon juice
1 onion, unpeeled, halved
1 carrot, cut into 3 pieces
2 sticks celery, cut into 3 pieces
2 sprigs thyme
1 teaspoon white peppercorns
2 fresh or dried bay leaves

Place all the ingredients in a large stainless-steel stockpot and cover with cold water, as slow heating helps bring out the flavours. The water should cover the bones by approximately 5 cm, still leaving a little room at the top of the pan. Cover with the lid and bring to the boil. Reduce the heat to low and simmer for a minimum of 12 and maximum of 24 hours. (I prefer a low and slow cook time to extract the nutrients from the bones.)

Occasionally skim off any fat or foam that rises to the surface and top up with additional water as needed to keep the ingredients covered.

Strain the broth through a fine-mesh sieve into a bowl and discard the solids. Once the broth has cooled, fat will rise to the surface. When this hardens, you can discard it.

The stock will keep for 5 days in the refrigerator or may be frozen in an airtight container for up to 6 months. (I like to freeze it in silicone ice cube trays, so it is easy to add a burst of flavour to whatever I'm cooking.)

Fish broth

MAKES ABOUT 2 LITRES
5 MINUTES PREPARATION
30 MINUTES COOKING

---

1 kg fish bones, rinsed, chopped into 2 cm pieces
(ask your fishmonger to chop them)
2 tablespoons apple cider vinegar
(see page 194) or lemon juice
1 onion, unpeeled, halved
1 carrot, cut into 3 pieces
2 sticks celery, cut into 3 pieces
2 sprigs thyme
1 teaspoon white peppercorns
2 fresh or dried bay leaves

Place all the ingredients in a large stainless-steel stockpot and cover with cold water, as slow heating helps bring out the flavours. The water should cover the bones by approximately 5 cm, still leaving a little room at the top of the pan. Cover with the lid and bring to the boil. Reduce the heat to low and simmer for 30 minutes. Occasionally skim off any foam that rises to the surface and top up with additional water as needed to keep the ingredients covered.

Strain the broth through a fine-mesh sieve into a bowl and discard the solids. Once the broth has cooled, fat will rise to the surface. When this hardens, you can discard it.

The stock will keep for 5 days in the refrigerator or may be frozen in an airtight container for up to 6 months. (I like to freeze it in silicone ice cube trays, so it is easy to add a burst of flavour to whatever I'm cooking.)

Vegetable stock

MAKES ABOUT 2 LITRES
5 MINUTES PREPARATION
4 HOURS COOKING

---

1 onion, unpeeled, halved

1 leek, well washed and roughly chopped

1 carrot, cut into 3 pieces

2 sticks celery, cut into 3 pieces

2 sprigs thyme

1 teaspoon white peppercorns

2 fresh or dried bay leaves

Place all the ingredients in a large stainless-steel stockpot and cover with cold water. The water should cover the vegetables by approximately 5 cm, still leaving a little room at the top of the pan. Cover with the lid and bring to the boil, then reduce the heat to low and simmer for 4 hours, skimming off any foam that rises to the surface. Strain the broth through a fine-mesh sieve, discarding the solids, then leave to cool.

The stock will keep for 5 days in the refrigerator or may be frozen in an airtight container for up to 6 months. (I like to freeze it in silicone ice cube trays, so it is easy to add a burst of flavour to whatever I'm cooking.)

Soups

There are many reasons I love soups; they are quick, simple, healthy, easy to digest and the ultimate comfort food. Plus, they are perfect for a weeknight meal, as they require little work from our digestive system before we go to sleep and there is only one pot to wash up – what more could a girl ask for?

Bouillabaisse

Bouillabaisse was definitely a stand-out dish for me during my training at Le Cordon Bleu in London. This is my version of the classic French dish – you can use your favourite seafood (prawns, scallops and mussels also work well).

4 vine-ripened tomatoes, scored at each end
ice cubes
1 tablespoon ghee (see page 194)
1 tablespoon Garlic Paste (see page 180)
1 leek, white part only, well washed,
    thinly sliced
1 onion, finely chopped
1 carrot, finely chopped
1 stick celery, finely chopped
$1/_2$ bulb fennel, thinly sliced
50 ml Cognac (optional)
2 litres Fish Broth (see page 34)
3 fresh or dried bay leaves
1 star anise
1 sprig thyme
pinch of saffron threads
1 tablespoon tomato paste (puree)
400 g fish fillets (I use a mixture of kingfish,
    barramundi and snapper), skin-off, pin-boned
100 g black mussels, bearded (see page 147)
torn flat-leaf parsley, to serve

Place the scored tomatoes in a bowl of boiling water for 30 seconds or until the skins start to peel. Remove and submerge in iced water, then peel. Dice and set aside.

Heat the ghee in a heavy-based saucepan over medium heat. Add the garlic, leek, onion, carrot, celery and fennel and cook for 8–10 minutes or until soft and translucent. Add the Cognac and increase the heat to high, then simmer until reduced and almost evaporated. Add the broth, bay leaves, star anise, thyme, saffron and tomato paste and bring to the boil. Reduce the heat to low and simmer for 30 minutes. Add the fish and mussels and poach for 5–7 minutes or until the fish is opaque and the mussels have opened. Stir in the reserved tomato.

To serve, divide among 4 bowls and scatter with parsley.

Flu-busting
chicken soup

SERVES 4–6 • 10 MINUTES PREPARATION •
1½ HOURS COOKING

This is probably the number one recipe in my repertoire because of its healthful qualities, and it is served year-round in my household for this very reason.

1 × 1.5 kg chicken
2 carrots, roughly chopped
2 sticks celery, roughly chopped
1 onion, sliced
1 teaspoon Garlic Paste (see page 180)
1 teaspoon Ginger Paste (see page 180)
1 star anise (optional)
1 teaspoon black peppercorns
2 litres Chicken Broth (see page 33) or water
handful fresh shiitake mushrooms, sliced
1 tablespoon fish sauce (optional)
sea salt and freshly ground black pepper
extra virgin olive oil, for drizzling
2 spring onions, trimmed, finely chopped

Place the chicken, carrot, celery, onion, garlic, ginger and spices in a large heavy-based saucepan and cover with chicken broth or water, then bring to the boil. Turn the heat down to low and simmer for 1½ hours, skimming the surface every now and again. Add the shiitake mushrooms and fish sauce (if using) for the last 10 minutes. Remove the chicken and, when cool enough to handle, coarsely shred the meat, discarding the bones and skin, then divide among 4 bowls.

Season the soup with salt and pepper, then remove the mushrooms and set aside. Strain the soup through a fine-mesh sieve, discarding the solids.

To serve, ladle the soup evenly into the 4 bowls, adding a few mushrooms, then drizzle with olive oil, scatter with spring onion and serve.

Chilled asparagus soup

I like to serve this garnished with a chilli sambal, made by frying shaved garlic, onion and chilli. The soup needs to be refrigerated for at least 2 hours before serving, or you can make it the day before.

1 tablespoon ghee (see page 194)
1 onion, finely chopped
1 teaspoon Garlic Paste (see page 180)
1 teaspoon Ginger Paste (see page 180)
1 fresh green chilli, finely chopped
2 cups (500ml) Chicken Broth (see page 33)
    or Vegetable Stock (see page 35)
18 spears (about 3 bunches) asparagus, trimmed,
    cut into 2 cm lengths
200 ml coconut cream
sea salt and freshly ground black pepper

Heat the ghee in a heavy-based saucepan over medium heat. Add the onion and cook for 4–6 minutes or until soft and translucent. Add the garlic, ginger and chilli and cook for 2 minutes.

Add the broth, increase the heat to high and bring immediately to the boil, then add the asparagus and cook for 5 minutes or until tender – you want to cook the asparagus quickly and cool the soup straightaway to retain its vibrant green colour. (If you cook the asparagus for too long, the soup will turn brown.)

Transfer the soup to a blender, then add the coconut cream and season to taste with salt and pepper. Blend until completely smooth, then chill in the fridge for 2 hours or until chilled.

To serve, divide among 4 bowls.

Chilled beetroot soup

SERVES 4 • 5 MINUTES PREPARATION + 2 HOURS CHILLING •
20 MINUTES COOKING

This can also be served warm, but I prefer it chilled for a fresh summer soup.

1 tablespoon ghee (see page 194)

1 onion, finely chopped

1 clove garlic, roughly chopped

4 beetroot, peeled, cut into 2 cm dice

1 sprig thyme

2 litres Beef Broth (see page 33), Chicken Broth
(see page 33) or Vegetable Stock (see page 35)

sea salt and freshly ground black pepper

Beetroot Chutney (see page 183), Homemade
Yoghurt (see page 181) or natural Greek-style
yoghurt and baby cress or micro-herbs, to serve

Heat the ghee in a heavy-based saucepan over low–medium heat. Add the onion and garlic and cook for 8–10 minutes or until soft and translucent. Add the beetroot, thyme and broth and bring to the boil. Season lightly with salt and pepper, then reduce the heat to low and simmer gently for 7–10 minutes or until the beetroot is tender.

Transfer the soup to a blender and blend until completely smooth, then press through a fine-mesh sieve; taste and adjust the seasoning if necessary.

Chill the soup in the fridge for 2 hours or until chilled.

To serve, divide among 4 bowls, then top with grated beetroot chutney, a dollop of yoghurt and cress or micro-herbs.

Celery and split pea soup

My mum rated a celery soup she had in a small family-owned restaurant in Tuscany, Italy, as one of the best dishes of the trip. I created this for her and she loves it.

2 tablespoons ghee (see page 194)

1 leek, white part only, well washed, thinly sliced

8 sticks celery, roughly chopped

1 onion, sliced

1 teaspoon Garlic Paste (see page 180)

1 cup (200 g) split peas, rinsed well, drained

1 litre Chicken Broth (see page 33), Vegetable Stock (see page 35) or Beef Broth (see page 33)

50 ml pouring cream

sea salt and freshly ground black pepper

celery leaves, flat-leaf parsley leaves, coconut milk, fish roe and crusty bread, to serve

Heat the ghee in a large heavy-based saucepan over medium heat. Add the leek, celery, onion and garlic and cook for 10–12 minutes or until very tender; add a dash of water to the pan if needed to stop them from browning. Add the split peas and broth and bring to a simmer, then reduce the heat to low, cover and simmer for 1 hour or until the split peas are very tender.

Transfer the soup to a blender, add the cream and blend until a smooth puree forms, then season to taste with salt and pepper.

To serve, divide among 4 bowls, then scatter with celery leaves and parsley, add a drizzle of coconut milk and a teaspoon or so of fish roe. I like to offer crusty bread alongside.

Chicken and soba noodle soup

Thin, brownish-grey soba noodles, made from buckwheat, are enormously popular in Japan, where they are prepared year-round. There, on hot summer days the noodles are eaten cold, arranged on a bamboo lattice rack with a dipping sauce, while on chilly winter days the noodles are immersed in piping hot broth. Soba noodles are available fresh and dried in Japanese markets; the dried variety may also be found in larger supermarkets. Look for miso paste in the same places. You can add cooked chicken strips for an extra hit of protein.

90 g soba noodles (see page 194)
1 tablespoon ghee (see page 194)
2 carrots, cut into thin strips
$^1/_4$ daikon (white radish), cut into thin strips
1 onion, thinly sliced
1 litre Chicken Broth (see page 33)
1 litre water
$^1/_4$ cup (70 g) white (shiro) miso (see page 195)
1 teaspoon Ginger Paste (see page 180)
6 nori (seaweed) sheets (see page 195),
  cut into 10 cm × 2 cm strips
2 cups (2 large handfuls) baby spinach
2 spring onions, thinly sliced on the diagonal
thinly sliced small fresh red chilli, to serve

Bring a large saucepan of water to the boil over high heat. Add the noodles and cook for 3 minutes or until just tender. Drain and set aside.

Place the ghee, carrot, daikon and onion in a large heavy-based saucepan over medium–high heat and cook for 1 minute. Whisk together the broth, water, miso and ginger and add to the pan. Bring to a simmer, then reduce the heat to medium and simmer for 3 minutes or until the miso has dissolved.

Add the nori and spinach and cook for 1 minute or until slightly softened but the spinach is still bright green. Add the spring onion.

To serve, using tongs, divide the noodles evenly among 4 warmed bowls, then ladle in the soup. Scatter with chopped chilli, then serve immediately.

Fish curry with roti

SERVES 4 • 20 MINUTES PREPARATION • 50 MINUTES COOKING

This dish is one of my all-time favourites and is a total show-stopper. There are a few different steps, but is absolutely worth the effort.

1 teaspoon shrimp paste

3 vine-ripened tomatoes, scored

ice cubes

1/4 cup (60 ml) sesame oil

2 onions, finely chopped

1 tablespoon Garlic Paste (see page 180)

1 tablespoon Ginger Paste (see page 180)

1 stalk lemongrass, white part only, finely chopped

1/2 teaspoon fenugreek seeds or fresh fenugreek

3 teaspoons finely chopped fresh turmeric
   or 1 teaspoon ground turmeric

1 teaspoon sweet paprika

1 teaspoon chilli powder

2 cups (500 ml) coconut milk

2 sprigs fresh curry leaves

2 tablespoons tamarind puree, or to taste

2 tablespoons fish sauce, or to taste

2 tablespoons honey, or to taste

2 firm white fish fillets, such as coral trout
   or barramundi (about 225 g each), skin on

juice of 1 lime, or to taste

fresh Roti (see page 178) or brown rice, crisp fried
   shallot (optional) and thinly sliced long fresh red
   chilli, to serve

Preheat the oven to 180°C (160°C fan-forced).

Wrap the shrimp paste in foil and roast for 5–10 minutes or until fragrant, then set aside.

Meanwhile, place the tomatoes in a saucepan of boiling water for 1 minute or until the skins split, then drain and transfer to a bowl of iced water to cool. Peel and discard the skin, then finely chop and set aside.

Heat the sesame oil in a wok or large heavy-based saucepan over medium heat. Add the onion, garlic, ginger and lemongrass and cook for 10 minutes or until softened. Add the fenugreek, turmeric, paprika, chilli and shrimp paste and cook for 1–2 minutes or until fragrant, then add the coconut milk, curry leaves, tamarind, fish sauce, honey and tomato and cook for another 18–20 minutes, stirring occasionally for the flavours to meld.

Add the fish and cook over low heat for 4–6 minutes or until cooked through, breaking the fillets up slightly with a wooden spoon. Add the lime juice and adjust the seasoning with extra tamarind, fish sauce and/or honey, if needed, to suit your taste.

To serve, ladle the soup into 4 bowls and serve with fresh roti or brown rice alongside, scattered with fried shallot, if using, and chilli.

Chicken, tomato and lentil soup

SERVES 6 • 15 MINUTES PREPARATION + 2–3 HOURS COOLING • 1 HOUR COOKING

For this recipe, and any other type of chicken soup, buy good-quality chicken stock or make your own (see page 33). Ras el hanout, a Moroccan spice blend, is available from Middle Eastern food stores and select delicatessens. Black lentils are also available from select delicatessens; if they're unavailable, substitute small green lentils.

1 × 1.6 kg chicken
1 litre Chicken Broth (see page 33)
1 litre water
sea salt and freshly ground black pepper
ghee (see page 194), for cooking
1 large onion, finely chopped
2 teaspoons Garlic Paste (see page 180)
2 teaspoons Ginger Paste (see page 180)
2 teaspoons ras el hanout (see page 195)
100 g cherry tomatoes, halved
180 g black lentils, rinsed
260 g cabbage, shredded
pinch of saffron threads
sea salt and freshly ground black pepper
$^1/_4$ cup (small handful) finely chopped
   flat-leaf parsley
Homemade Yoghurt (see page 181) or natural
   Greek-style yoghurt, drained, thinly sliced
   small red chilli and crusty bread, to serve

Place the chicken in a heavy-based saucepan large enough to fit it snugly, then add the broth and water (or enough to just cover). Season to taste with salt and pepper and bring to the boil over medium–high heat. Reduce the heat to low–medium, cover and simmer for 10 minutes. Leave the chicken in the pan of stock to cool to room temperature (2–3 hours). Remove the chicken and coarsely shred the meat, discarding the bones and skin, then set aside. Strain the stock, discarding the solids. Set 1 litre of the stock aside (freeze the remainder for another use).

Heat the ghee in a heavy-based saucepan over medium–high heat. Add the onion and cook for 5–10 minutes or until tender, then add the garlic, ginger and ras el hanout and stir for 1–2 minutes or until fragrant. Add the tomato, lentils, cabbage, saffron and reserved stock, then season to taste with salt and pepper and bring to the boil. Reduce the heat to medium and simmer for 25–30 minutes or until the lentils are tender. Add the parsley, season to taste and stir in the chicken, then simmer for a few minutes to warm through.

To serve, ladle the soup into 4 bowls, top with a dollop of yoghurt, scatter with chilli and serve with crusty bread alongside.

Salads

Salads are so wonderfully variable and versatile; you are only limited by your imagination. Hot or cold, offered as a main or a side, with fruit or vegetables, with nuts and seeds or protein; I could go on and on. The combination of taste and textures, teamed with a zingy dressing, will tantalise your senses.

Perfect for any meal, salads are far more than leafy greens – using seasonal produce is the key. I've loved putting together the following recipes for you. When entertaining, place a colourful selection of salads on the table for sharing – you eliminate the need for a centrepiece and will have your guests salivating.

Winter green and white bean salad with mint and olives

SERVES 4 • 10 MINUTES PREPARATION • 5 MINUTES COOKING

Winter greens, mint, lemon zest and olives all have an aspect of bitterness, which is probably why they work so well together. Mild, creamy white beans soften the robust flavours in this perfect-for-late-autumn salad. This also keeps well in the fridge for midweek lunches.

3 large handfuls (3 cups) bitter winter greens such as dandelion leaves, wild rocket or frisee, stems discarded
sea salt
1 × 400 g tin cannellini beans, drained, rinsed
¹/₂ small onion, finely diced
8 pitted green olives, sliced
¹/₄ cup (small handful) mint leaves
freshly ground black pepper

LEMON DRESSING
¹/₃ cup (80 ml) extra virgin olive oil
1 teaspoon finely grated lemon zest
2 tablespoons lemon juice

Cook the greens (except for rocket, if using) in a large heavy-based saucepan of salted boiling water for 4 minutes or until tender. Drain and leave to cool, then lightly squeeze out the excess water. Roughly chop the greens.

To make the dressing, place the olive oil, lemon zest and lemon juice in a small bowl and whisk to combine. Set aside.

Place the greens, cannellini beans, onion, olives and mint in a large shallow bowl, then stir well to combine. Spoon over the dressing, season with salt and pepper, then divide among 4 bowls and serve.

Prawn and soba noodle salad with sesame-ginger dressing

SERVES 4 • 10 MINUTES PREPARATION • 10 MINUTES COOKING

I am a big fan of soba noodles. Made from buckwheat flour, they are easier to digest than wheat-based noodles, which is why I like to use them in an evening meal, but they are also great for lunch. Sometimes I add baby spinach leaves to this, if I have them in my fridge.

270 g soba noodles (see page 194)
24 raw prawns, peeled and cleaned
    with tails intact
1 teaspoon Garlic Paste (see page 180)
sea salt and freshly ground black pepper
1 tablespoon olive oil
1 Lebanese (small) cucumber, diced
2 spring onions, thinly sliced on the diagonal
$^1/_4$ cup (small handful) coriander, roughly torn
toasted sesame seeds (optional) and Chilli Salt
    (see page 187), to serve

SESAME-GINGER DRESSING
50 ml light soy sauce
$1^1/_2$ tablespoons rice wine vinegar
1 tablespoon extra virgin olive oil
$1^1/_2$ teaspoons hulled tahini
$^1/_2$ teaspoon finely grated ginger

Cook the soba in a large saucepan of boiling water for 2–4 minutes or until just tender. Drain and refresh under cold running water, then place in a large bowl.

Coat the prawns in the garlic paste and season with salt and pepper. Heat the olive oil in a large heavy-based frying pan over medium–high heat and sear the prawns for 1–2 minutes on each side or until just cooked through.

For the dressing, place all the ingredients in a small bowl and whisk together until smooth (or pop all the ingredients into a small jar, seal with the lid and shake). Set aside.

To serve, pour the dressing over the noodles and add the cucumber and spring onion, then toss to combine. Top with the prawns and scatter with the coriander, sesame seed, if using, and chilli salt.

Broccoli and pickled onion salad with avocado, chilli and lime dressing

SERVES 4 • 20 MINUTES PREPARATION + COOLING TIME • 20 MINUTES COOKING

This is a hidden gem; it's incredibly tasty and is also packed with loads of nutrients. These are the kind of dishes I love eating as you don't realise just how healthy they are.

1 cup (170 g) cracked buckwheat (see page 194), soaked in cold water for 30 minutes

2 heads broccoli, cut into small florets

ice cubes

$^1/_4$ cup (40 g) pine nuts

$^1/_2$ cup (60 g) chopped pecans

$^1/_4$ cup (35 g) raisins

1 quantity Pickled Onion (see page 183)

50 g feta, crumbled

sea salt and freshly ground black pepper

baby basil leaves (optional) and micro mustard cress (optional), to serve

AVOCADO, CHILLI AND LIME DRESSING

1 ripe avocado, seeded, flesh scooped out

finely grated zest and juice of 1 lemon

1 tablespoon aged red wine vinegar

1 tablespoon honey

$^1/_2$ fresh green chilli, finely chopped

$^1/_2$ cup (handful) basil leaves

sea salt and freshly ground black pepper

Drain the buckwheat and place in a heavy-based saucepan, then cover with water and boil for 10 minutes. Place a metal steamer basket on top, then add the broccoli and steam for 5 minutes or until just tender but still with a crunch. Cool immediately in ice cold water. Drain and set aside. Leave the buckwheat to cool in the pan to room temperature.

Heat a small frying pan over medium heat, then dry-fry the pine nuts for 1 minute or until they are slightly golden. Set aside to cool.

Place the buckwheat, broccoli, pine nuts, pecans and raisins in a large bowl and mix well.

Drain the pickled onion and discard the vinegar. Add the onion to the salad and stir, then transfer to a platter.

For the dressing, place all the ingredients in a blender and blend on medium speed for 30 seconds or until smooth. Drizzle the dressing over the salad.

To serve, scatter over the feta, basil and mustard cress, if using, and lightly toss, then season to taste.

Brown rice salad with mint and coriander dressing

SERVES 4 • 5 MINUTES PREPARATION • 15 MINUTES COOKING

I love finding ways to create beautiful dressings without the nasty high-fat elements. This dressing is both delicious and nutritious. This is a great way to use leftover cooked rice, if you happen to have some in your fridge.

1 cup (200 g) brown rice

2 cups (500 ml) Chicken Broth (see page 33) or water

100 g fresh or frozen green peas

$^1/_4$ cup (35 g) mixed unsalted nuts

$^1/_4$ cup (35 g) mixed seeds, such as sesame, sunflower and pumpkin seeds (pepitas)

MINT AND CORIANDER DRESSING

1 cup (1 large handful) coriander roots, well washed

1 cup (1 large handful) mint

1 lemon, juiced and zest finely grated

1 lime, juiced and zest finely grated

200 g Homemade Yoghurt (see page 181) or natural Greek-style yoghurt

sea salt and freshly ground black pepper

Cook the brown rice in the chicken broth or water in a heavy-based saucepan following the packet instructions for 15 minutes or until al dente. Set aside to cool.

Blanch the peas in a saucepan of simmering water, then drain and set aside.

For the dressing, place the coriander root, mint leaves, lemon and lime juice and zest and yoghurt in a blender. Season well with salt and pepper, then blend until well combined.

To serve, place the rice, peas, nuts and seeds in a bowl, add the dressing and mix together well.

Beetroot and walnut salad

I'm a big fan of keeping salads simple – pick an ingredient and make that the main element of the dish. Beetroot and walnut are the perfect co-stars here.

1 bunch each purple and golden baby beetroot, scrubbed (if they aren't available, use regular baby beetroot)

$^{1}/_{3}$ cup (80 ml) extra virgin olive oil

sea salt

$^{1}/_{2}$ cup (50 g) walnuts

pinch of cayenne pepper

1 pomegranate, seeds removed

2 wedges preserved lemon, flesh removed and discarded, rind cut into julienne

1 cup (large handful) flat-leaf parsley, roughly chopped

handful (about ½ cup) basil

freshly ground black pepper

$1^{1}/_{2}$ tablespoons aged red wine vinegar

1 golden shallot, finely chopped

basil and micro cress, to garnish

100 g ricotta salata (see page 195) or 150 g goat's cheese

Preheat the oven to 180°C (160°C fan-forced).

Individually wrap the beetroot in foil, with a drizzle of the olive oil and sprinkle of sea salt, then roast for 45–50 minutes or until tender. Remove from the oven, discard the foil and halve the beetroot.

Meanwhile, scatter the walnuts over a baking tray and sprinkle the cayenne over, then roast in the oven for 8 minutes or until golden brown. Set aside to cool.

Combine the beetroot, pomegranate seeds, lemon rind, herbs and walnuts in a bowl, then season to taste with salt and pepper and spread over a serving platter.

Whisk the vinegar and remaining olive oil together in a small bowl, add the shallot and drizzle over the salad.

To serve, scatter the salad with basil and micro cress, then finely grate ricotta salata or crumble goat's cheese over the top.

Moroccan freekeh and nut salad

A great side dish to serve with a piece of seared steak or grilled chicken. You could easily use brown rice instead of freekeh, if you prefer.

$1/_2$ cup (90 g) cracked freekeh (see page 194)

5 dried Turkish apricots, finely chopped

$1/_4$ cup (40 g) blanched almonds

$1/_2$ cup (80 g) pumpkin seed kernels (pepitas)

$1/_4$ cup (35 g) sunflower seed kernels

$1/_4$ cup (35 g) slivered almonds

2 tablespoons pine nuts

$1/_4$ cup (35 g) sultanas

$1/_4$ cup (40 g) Craisins (dried cranberries)

1 pomegranate, seeds removed

2 tablespoons extra virgin olive oil

$1/_2$ teaspoon sea salt

1 cup (large handful) flat-leaf parsley, roughly chopped

3 teaspoons pomegranate molasses (see page 195)

$1/_3$ cup (60 g) unsalted shelled pistachios

unsprayed rose petals (optional), to serve

lemon slices (optional), to serve

Cook the freekeh in a heavy-based saucepan of boiling water for 20 minutes or until tender. Drain and rinse under cold water, then transfer to a salad bowl and set aside.

Meanwhile, place the apricots, seeds and nuts in a heavy-based non-stick frying pan and gently dry-roast for 1–2 minutes or until golden. Immediately remove from the heat, ensuring they do not burn, then set aside to cool.

Add the sultanas, craisins and three-quarters of the pomegranate seeds to the freekeh. Stir through with 1 tablespoon of the olive oil and the salt, then stir in the parsley. Add the cooled nut and seed mixture and stir through. Drizzle with the pomegranate molasses and remaining olive oil and stir to combine.

Just before serving, add most of the rose petals (if using) and mix in. Top with the remaining pomegranate seeds, pistachios, rose petals and lemon slices, if using, then serve.

Spiced cauliflower and chickpea salad

SERVES 4 • 20 MINUTES PREPARATION + OVERNIGHT SOAKING •
2 HOURS COOKING

I visit India often and am always amazed and inspired by the creative use of cauliflower in their recipes. This dish, in particular, is super-tasty.

$^1/_4$ cup (50 g) dried chickpeas

1 litre water

pinch of bicarbonate of soda

sea salt and freshly ground black pepper

1 cauliflower, broken into small florets

50 ml extra virgin olive oil

1 red onion, thinly sliced

1 tablespoon ground cumin

1 tablespoon brown mustard seeds

2 teaspoons fennel seeds

1 teaspoon ground turmeric

1 teaspoon ground coriander

1 teaspoon ground ginger

1 teaspoon smoked paprika

$^1/_4$ teaspoon ground cinnamon

4 cloves

2 cardamom pods

$^1/_4$ cup (35 g) hazelnuts

50 g baby spinach

$^1/_2$ cup (handful) coriander, roughly torn

$^1/_2$ cup (handful) mint leaves

$^1/_4$ cup (35 g) raisins, soaked in $\frac{1}{2}$ cup
(125 ml) hot water

$^1/_2$ lemon

100 g Labneh (see page 181)

Soak the chickpeas in the water overnight with the bicarbonate of soda. Drain and rinse well, then place in a heavy-based saucepan, cover with fresh water and bring to the boil. Reduce the heat to low and simmer for 1½ hours minutes or until tender, skimming off any froth from the surface. Drain and season to taste with salt and pepper.

Preheat the oven to 180°C (160°C fan-forced).

Place the cauliflower florets in a metal steamer basket over a large saucepan of simmering water. Cook, covered, for 8 minutes or until just tender; make sure you don't take it too far as you will also be roasting the cauliflower and it will fall apart. Pat dry with paper towel and place on a large baking tray, then toss with half of the olive oil, the onion and all of the spices. Roast for 15 minutes or until caramelised, then discard the cloves and cardamom. Set aside to cool.

Meanwhile, roast the hazelnuts for 5 minutes. Remove and place on a clean tea towel, fold in half and rub off the skins. Discard the skins and chop the hazelnuts in half, then transfer to a large bowl.

Add the spinach, herbs, cauliflower and drained raisins and gently toss. Transfer to a serving bowl. Drizzle over the rest of the olive oil and squeeze fresh lemon juice on top. Serve with labneh or your choice of cheese.

Crab, green mango and mint salad

Puffed rice is an ingredient I have started using a lot in my cooking. It has a great texture, but be careful as it can go soggy if you leave it too long before serving.

4 coriander roots, well washed

finely grated zest and juice of 1 lemon

2 tablespoons mirin (Japanese rice cooking wine)

1 teaspoon honey

sea salt and freshly ground black pepper

1 green mango, peeled and thinly sliced

2 cups (70 g) puffed rice (see page 195)

¹/₂ cup (70 g) unsalted peanuts

1 long fresh red chilli, seeded and thinly sliced

300 g cooked crabmeat, picked, plus extra to serve

betel leaves, mint leaves and torn coriander, to serve

Blend the coriander root, lemon zest and juice, mirin, honey and salt and pepper to taste in a blender until smooth, then set aside.

Mix together the mango, puffed rice, peanuts, red chilli and half of the crabmeat in a bowl and stir to combine.

Place the betel leaves on 4 plates. Add the desired amount of dressing to the crab mixture and serve immediately to avoid the puffed rice going soggy. Top with extra crabmeat, chilli and mint and coriander.

Radish and seaweed with miso dressing

Seaweed is rich in calcium, magnesium, phosphorus, iron and potassium. You can buy fresh seaweed from Asian food stores or rehydrate dried versions. This goes perfectly with crisp-skin fish or mixed through some soba noodles. The dressing keeps well in the fridge for up to 2 weeks and is lovely over stir-fried greens. If not using tamari, then add a generous pinch of sea salt.

1 cup (large handful) fresh seaweed (or 2 teaspoons shredded dried seaweed) (see page 195)

2 tablespoons white sesame seeds

6 pink radishes, thinly sliced

2 spring onions, sliced on the diagonal

$^1/_4$ cup (small handful) coriander, roughly chopped

MISO DRESSING

1 tablespoon lime juice

$^1/_2$ teaspoon tamari (see page 195, optional)

$^1/_2$ teaspoon sesame oil

$^1/_2$ teaspoon honey

$^1/_2$ teaspoon apple cider vinegar (see page 194) or rice wine vinegar

1 teaspoon sweet white (shiro) miso paste (see page 195)

1 long fresh red chilli, thinly sliced

If using fresh seaweed, rinse it thoroughly a couple of times. If using dried seaweed, soak it in water for the recommended time on the packet. Drain, rinse and set aside.

Toast the sesame seeds in a small dry frying pan over medium heat for 30 seconds.

For the miso dressing, place the lime juice, tamari (if using), sesame oil, honey, vinegar, miso paste and chilli in a jar and shake well until emulsified. Set aside. (Makes about $^1/_4$ cup [60ml].)

Place the seaweed, radish and spring onion in a bowl, pour over the desired amount of dressing and toss. Divide among 4 bowls and top with the coriander and toasted sesame seeds, then serve.

Tomato salad with burrata and crostini

SERVES 4 • 5 MINUTES PREPARATION • 5 MINUTES COOKING

This classic combination is hard to pass up when tomatoes are at their peak, and it's one of my favourite summer snacks. Serve the burrata at room temperature to get the most from its luscious milkiness.

250 g mixed baby heirloom tomatoes, halved
250 g mixed tomatoes, halved if desired
4 burrata (see page 91), at room temperature, torn
$^1/_4$ cup (60 ml) extra virgin olive oil
3 teaspoons red wine vinegar
sea salt and freshly ground black pepper
micro basil, to serve

CROSTINI
8 thin baguette slices
olive oil, for brushing
$^1/_2$ clove garlic

For the crostini, heat a chargrill pan over high heat. Brush the baguette slices with olive oil and chargrill, turning occasionally, for 2–4 minutes or until golden and crisp. Rub each crostini with the cut side of the garlic and set aside. Tear roughly.

Scatter the tomato, crostini and burrata on a large platter. Whisk the olive oil and vinegar in a bowl to combine and season to taste with salt and pepper, then drizzle over the tomato salad.

To serve, scatter the salad with the micro basil.

Coleslaw

SERVES 4–6
10 MINUTES PREPARATION

This classic salad featured heavily in my childhood and still, to this day, every time I return home to Mackay, my nan makes a huge batch and brings it over. It makes a healthy snack and is absolutely delicious.

$1/_3$ red cabbage (about 500 g), shredded
$1/_3$ white cabbage (about 500 g), shredded
2 carrots, cut into julienne
2 golden shallots, thinly sliced
sea salt and freshly ground black pepper
1 cup (handful) flat-leaf parsley, coarsely torn
1 cup (handful) mint, coarsely torn
$1/_2$ cup (150 g) good-quality mayonnaise

Combine the cabbage, carrot and shallot in a large bowl, season with salt and pepper to taste and toss to mix well. Add the herbs and mayonnaise and toss to combine. Transfer to a serving bowl and serve.

Roast pumpkin, pomegranate and feta salad

SERVES 4
10 MINUTES PREPARATION
30 MINUTES COOKING

This is such a simple dish with so much flavour, and great to serve alongside meat.

ghee (see page 194), for cooking
1 kent pumpkin, cut into thin wedges, seeded, skin on
1 teaspoon ground cinnamon
1 sprig thyme, leaves finely chopped
sea salt and freshly ground black pepper
1 pomegranate, seeds removed
$1/_2$ cup (handful) flat-leaf parsley, torn
50 g feta

Preheat the oven to 180°C (160°C fan-forced).

Place the ghee in a shallow roasting pan, then add the pumpkin wedges and sprinkle with the cinnamon, thyme, salt and pepper. Roast for 30 minutes or until cooked through and slightly shrivelled.

Place on a serving plate, top with the pumpkin, the pomegranate seeds and parsley, then crumble the feta over and serve.

Watercress and halloumi salad

You can keep the scooped-out papaya seeds to add to smoothies or salad dressings – beware though, they taste like radish! Ask everyone to be seated before you fry the halloumi as this salad is best eaten when it is hot from the pan.

4 cups (4 large handfuls) watercress sprigs

200 g cherry or baby plum tomatoes, halved

1 red onion, thinly sliced

1 large ripe hass avocado, flesh scooped
    out, sliced

sea salt

handful of pine nuts (or pumpkin [pepita]
    or sunflower seeds)

1 teaspoon ghee (see page 194)

250 g halloumi, sliced

1 ripe papaya (or ½ large one), halved, seeded

extra virgin olive oil, for drizzling

honey, for drizzling

apple cider vinegar (see page 194)
    or lime or lemon juice

freshly ground black pepper

Take a large flat serving dish and distribute the watercress over it (you can roughly snip the stems a little for slightly more elegant eating).

Scatter the tomato, onion and avocado over the watercress and season with a little salt, if desired (not too much as the halloumi is salty, remember!).

Gently toast the pine nuts in a small dry frying pan over low heat for 5 minutes or until lightly golden and set aside.

Using a flattish spoon, scoop out thick slivers of the papaya flesh and pile them onto the salad; if you're struggling to make it look nice, try slicing or cubing the fruit.

Heat the ghee in a large heavy-based frying pan over high heat and lay down the halloumi slices without overcrowding (you might have to do this in batches if your pan is small). Pan-fry for 1 minute on each side or until golden brown – keep your eye on them! Immediately lay the halloumi across the salad.

At the table, sprinkle over the pine nuts, drizzle over a generous amount of olive oil and a little honey, add a splash of vinegar or juice and a good grinding of pepper, then tuck in.

Seared duck breast with charred fig and rocket salad

SERVES 4 • 10 MINUTES PREPARATION • 15 MINUTES COOKING

One of the joys of autumn is the arrival of figs. While I love to celebrate this glorious fruit by simply eating them with the skin on, they are also wonderful paired with a duck salad.

2 duck breast fillets, skin on
sea salt
6 figs, halved
freshly ground black pepper
200 g rocket or watercress sprigs, trimmed
4 spring onions, thinly sliced
1 red apple, cut into julienne
Classic Vinaigrette (see page 184),
   as needed

Season the duck breasts with sea salt all over. Place, skin-side down, in a clean, cold heavy-based frying pan and turn the heat on to low, then cook for 8–10 minutes or until the fat has mostly melted into a large pool in the pan; you want to cook the skin slowly in order to render the layer of fat between the skin and breast and make the skin crisp. Carefully pour the fat into a separate bowl (don't throw this away as it is perfect to use for roasting potatoes).

Flip the breasts over and cook for a further 2 minutes (this side is much quicker to cook). Remove the breasts from the pan, season with pepper and leave to rest for 5 minutes. Cut into 1 cm-thick slices.

Add the figs, cut-side down, to a dry heavy-based frying pan over high heat and char for 1 minute or until fragrant and slightly blackened. Set aside.

Combine the rocket, spring onion, apple and fig in a bowl. Pour over enough vinaigrette to just coat the ingredients, then toss.

To serve, divide the salad and sliced duck among 4 plates, and serve.

Puy lentil, oven-dried tomato and caramelised fennel salad

SERVES 4 • 15 MINUTES PREPARATION + COOLING TIME • 4 HOURS COOKING

Here is a simple way to have a stash of your own oven-dried tomatoes at home instead of buying them from the shops. Simply coat the tomatoes with spices and olive oil and roast in the oven on a low temperature to dry.

8 sprigs thyme

1 teaspoon sea salt

$^1/_2$ teaspoon fennel seeds

1 teaspoon Garlic Paste (see page 180)

1 tablespoon olive oil

400 g egg (plum) tomatoes, quartered

2 small bulbs fennel, quartered

1 red onion, thinly sliced

1 tablespoon red wine vinegar

250 g puy or other green lentils

$^1/_4$ cup (60 ml) extra virgin olive oil

small handful ($^1/_4$ cup) flat-leaf parsley, roughly chopped

80 g feta, crumbled or diced

freshly ground black pepper

Preheat the oven to 150°C (130°C fan-forced).

Place the thyme, salt, fennel seeds, garlic paste and olive oil in a bowl and toss to combine, then add the tomato and fennel and toss to coat. Place the tomato quarters skin-side down on a baking tray and roast for 4 hours; the longer you leave them, the more dried and sweet they will become. Thirty minutes before removing the tomato, add the fennel to the tray and continue to roast until the fennel is caramelised. Set aside to cool.

Meanwhile, place the onion, vinegar and salt to taste in a small bowl and leave to pickle until ready to serve.

Cook the lentils in a saucepan of boiling salted water for 20–30 minutes or until tender. Drain well and place in a large bowl. Add the warm tomato and fennel, stir in the olive oil, then leave to cool to room temperature.

To serve, add the parsley and feta and season with salt and pepper to taste. Divide among 4 bowls and serve.

Cucumber, fennel, hazelnut and caper salad

SERVES 4 • 10 MINUTES PREPARATION

A green machine of a salad. I use a mandoline to shave the cucumber and fennel, but if you don't have one, finely slice them with a sharp knife instead.

1 cup (140 g) hazelnuts

1 Lebanese (small) cucumber, thinly sliced lengthways with a mandoline

1 bulb fennel, thinly sliced with a mandoline

$^1/_4$ cup (50 g) capers in brine, drained

$^1/_4$ cup (small handful) dill, finely chopped

50 ml apple cider vinegar

50 ml extra virgin olive oil

$^1/_2$ lemon, juiced

sea salt and freshly ground black pepper

Preheat the oven to 180°C (160°C fan-forced).

Scatter the hazelnuts on a baking tray and roast for 5 minutes. Remove and place on a clean tea towel, fold in half and rub off the skins. Discard the skins and roughly chop.

Combine the cucumber, fennel, hazelnuts, capers and dill in a large bowl.

Place the vinegar, olive oil, lemon juice and salt and pepper to taste in a jar and shake to emulsify. Pour over the salad and toss to combine, then serve.

Scallop salad with ponzu dressing

SERVES 4 • 10 MINUTES PREPARATION • 10 MINUTES COOKING

The Japanese use ponzu sauce as a dipping sauce for raw fish, but it also works very well with other seafood, such as the scallops used in this recipe. Ponzu is traditionally made with Japanese lemons (yuzu), sometimes available in Australia, but limes may be substituted. Store ponzu dressing, covered, in the refrigerator, for up to two months; the flavour improves with age.

1 teaspoon fennel seeds

¹/₄ cup (3 tablespoons) ghee (see page 194)

2 cobs corn, kernels sliced off

2 cups (2 large handfuls) baby spinach leaves

6 spring onions, trimmed and thinly sliced

¹/₂ cup (handful) coriander leaves

16 scallops, roe off

sea salt and freshly ground black pepper

PONZU DRESSING

¹/₂ cup (6 tablespoons) bonito flakes

100 ml Fish Broth (see page 34)

¹/₄ cup (60 ml) lime juice

¹/₄ cup (60 ml) soy sauce

1¹/₂ teaspoons mirin (Japanese rice cooking wine)

For the ponzu dressing, place the bonito flakes, broth, lime juice, soy sauce and mirin in a small heavy-based saucepan and bring to the boil over high heat. Reduce the heat to medium and simmer for 1 minute. Remove from the heat and leave to cool, then strain into a bowl, discarding the solids. Set aside. (Makes about 1 cup [250ml].)

Toast the fennel seeds in a small dry frying pan over medium heat for 1–2 minutes or until aromatic. Grind to a powder with a mortar and pestle, then set aside.

Heat 1 tablespoon of the ghee in a heavy-based non-stick frying pan over medium–high heat. Add the corn and sauté for 5 minutes or until lightly golden. Transfer to a large bowl. Add the spinach, spring onion and coriander leaves to the bowl and toss with ½ cup (125 ml) of the ponzu dressing. Divide the salad among 4 plates.

Pat the scallops dry with paper towel, then rub with the remaining ghee and season with the ground fennel and salt and pepper to taste. Heat the frying pan over medium–high heat, then add the scallops, placing them in a clockwise direction starting at 12 o'clock; this ensures you remember the first scallop you added to the pan so you cook them evenly. Sear the scallops for 1½ minutes or until lightly browned underneath, then flip and cook the other side for 1 minute or until browned and they are just cooked through; do not overcook to ensure they are moist and tender.

To serve, arrange 4 scallops around each plate, then drizzle the salad with the remaining ponzu dressing.

Baked snapper with cucumber, ruby grapefruit and mint salad

SERVES 4 • 10 MINUTES PREPARATION • 20 MINUTES COOKING

I love creating simple dishes like this. Just pour your sauce on the fish, bake it in the oven and it's good to go. Here, I've used ruby grapefruit, but you could always use a regular grapefruit instead.

4 × 150 g snapper fillets, skin on, pin-boned

**CUCUMBER, RUBY GRAPEFRUIT
AND MINT SALAD**

1 large ruby grapefruit

50 ml fish sauce

50 ml soy sauce

50 ml honey

100 ml grapeseed oil

3 spring onions, thinly sliced on the diagonal, white and green parts set aside separately

10 mint leaves, roughly chopped (Vietnamese mint if you can find it)

1/4 cup (small handful) flat-leaf parsley, roughly chopped

1 fresh red birds eye chilli, finely chopped

2 Lebanese (small) cucumbers, shaved using a mandoline

1/2 cup (handful) coriander leaves, chopped

Preheat the oven to 220°C (200°C fan-forced).

Arrange the snapper fillets in a baking dish so that none are touching.

For the salad, using a sharp knife, slice the top and bottom off the grapefruit, then slice off the skin including the white pith, starting from the top and working to the bottom. Working over a bowl to catch the juices, cut out the segments in between the frame, then set aside.

Strain the grapefruit juice through a fine-mesh sieve into a small bowl and whisk in the fish sauce, soy sauce, honey and grapeseed oil.

Spoon half the dressing over the fish, then pop the fish into the oven and bake for 15–18 minutes or until just cooked through.

Meanwhile, place the green part of the spring onion in the remaining dressing, then add the mint, parsley, chilli and grapefruit segments and set aside.

Just before serving, add the cucumber, coriander and the white part of the spring onion to the bowl of salad.

To serve, arrange the salad around a large shallow serving bowl or platter. Flake or cut the snapper into bite-sized pieces. Place the snapper evenly on top, drizzle with as much dressing as you desire, then serve straight away.

Moroccan-inspired quinoa salad with ras el hanout

SERVES 4 • 15 MINUTES PREPARATION • 30 MINUTES COOKING

If you don't feel like marinating the zucchini and eggplant yourself, you can find them ready-made in jars from the deli section of most supermarkets (but nothing beats homemade).

1 cup (160 g) blanched almonds
sea salt
1 zucchini (courgette), thinly sliced
1 eggplant (aubergine), thinly sliced
olive oil, for cooking and drizzling
1 teaspoon Garlic Paste (see page 180)
freshly ground black pepper
1½ cups (285 g) quinoa (see page 195), rinsed
1 tablespoon ras el hanout (see page 195)
2 cups (500 ml) Chicken Broth
    (see page 33) or water
juice of ½ lemon
¼ cup (60 ml) extra virgin olive oil
¼ cup (35 g) raisins
2 cups (2 large handfuls) mint,
    roughly chopped
1 cup (1 large handful) coriander,
    roughly chopped
2 avocados, peeled, seeded, cut
    into 2 cm dice
4 small spring onions, finely chopped
lemon cheeks, to serve

Preheat the oven to 180°C (160°C fan-forced). Heat the barbecue grill plate, or chargrill pan on high heat.

Scatter the almonds on a baking tray and roast for 5 minutes or until golden. Transfer to a bowl and season with salt.

Brush the zucchini and eggplant with olive oil, then barbecue or chargrill for 4 minutes on each side or until you see char marks; try not to move them around too much when checking, as you want the char marks to be even. Transfer to a bowl, drizzle with olive oil, then add the garlic, season with salt and pepper and set aside.

Place the quinoa, ras el hanout and chicken broth or water in a heavy-based saucepan, then bring to simmer, reduce the heat to low and cook for 12 minutes or until tender with a gentle crunch. Transfer to a large bowl and add the lemon juice, olive oil, raisins and half of the mint and coriander. Toss thoroughly to combine.

To serve, divide the quinoa mixture among 4 bowls, along with the marinated vegetables, avocado and spring onion. Scatter with the remaining mint and coriander and the roasted almonds, then serve with a lemon cheek in each bowl.

Yoghurt-marinated chicken with quinoa and rocket salad

SERVES 2 • 10 MINUTES PREPARATION • 20 MINUTES COOKING

This is a really healthy way to add flavour to one of my favourite quick cooking cuts, chicken breast fillets.

2 chicken breast fillets, cut into 2 cm-thick slices
150 g quinoa (see page 195)
100 g rocket
large handful flat-leaf parsley, roughly chopped
50 g pumpkin seeds (pepitas)
50 g raisins

YOGHURT MARINADE

1 small fresh red chilli, finely chopped
$^1/_2$ cup (140 g) Homemade Yoghurt (see page 181)
   or natural Greek-style yoghurt
2 cloves garlic, roughly chopped
1 teaspoon ground turmeric
1 teaspoon ground cumin
sea salt and freshly ground black pepper
olive oil, for drizzling
juice of 1 lemon

POMEGRANATE DRESSING

balsamic vinegar, for drizzling
extra virgin olive oil, for drizzling
1 teaspoon dijon mustard
1 tablespoon pomegranate molasses
   (see page 195)

For the marinade, place the chilli, yoghurt, garlic, turmeric, cumin, salt and pepper to taste, olive oil and the lemon juice in a blender and blend until it forms a very smooth consistency. If it's too thick, add a little more olive oil and/or lemon juice. Place the chicken in a glass or ceramic dish, then pour the marinade over and turn to coat. Leave to marinate for 30 minutes in the fridge.

Meanwhile, cook the quinoa in a saucepan of simmering water following the packet instructions. Drain and leave to cool.

For the dressing, combine all the ingredients in a small bowl. Set aside.

Preheat the oven to 180°C (160°C fan-forced).

Place the chicken and all the marinade on a baking tray lined with foil, then bake for 15 minutes or until just cooked through. Leave to rest and cool. Cut into thick slices.

Transfer the quinoa to a large bowl, then add the rocket, parsley, pumpkin seeds and raisins and stir to combine. Drizzle over the dressing.

To serve, divide the quinoa and rocket salad among plates, then top with the chicken.

Slow-cooked turkey with superfood salad of kale, beetroot pickle, avocado, tomatoes and soy-ginger dressing

SERVES 4 • 10 MINUTES PREPARATION + PICKLING TIME

This dish is so vibrant and flavoursome, and so pretty, considering it can be thrown together in 10 minutes. Leftovers don't need to be boring – this is definitely my go-to meal.

400 g leftover **Slow-roasted Turkey** (see page 103), shredded

200 g kale, finely shredded

1 avocado, flesh scooped out, diced

200 g mixed heirloom cherry tomatoes, halved

BEETROOT PICKLE

1 bunch baby beetroot, thinly sliced widthways

2 star anise

4 cloves

$^1/_2$ cup (125 ml) mirin (Japanese rice cooking wine)

$^1/_2$ cup (125 ml) shao hsing rice wine

SOY-GINGER DRESSING

2 tablespoons sesame oil

1 tablespoon soy sauce

$^1/_2$ cup (125 ml) rice wine vinegar

1 onion, finely diced

$^1/_2$ teaspoon **Garlic Paste** (see page 180)

1 teaspoon finely grated ginger

2 teaspoons honey

For the pickle, combine all the ingredients in a small heavy-based saucepan, then bring to a simmer over medium–high heat. Remove from the heat, transfer to a sterilised jar and leave to cool.

For the dressing, place the oil, soy sauce, vinegar, onion, garlic, ginger and honey in a jar, then shake to mix; this will not completely emulsify. Set aside until ready to serve. (Makes about ¾ cup [180 ml]. Leftovers can be stored in the fridge for up to 1 week.)

Place the turkey, kale, drained beetroot pickle, avocado and tomato in a large bowl and stir gently to combine. Pour over the desired amount of dressing, then stir gently to coat and divide among 4 bowls (or pop into 4 containers to take to work for lunch).

Crispy-skin kingfish with broad bean, asparagus, pancetta and feta salad

SERVES 4 • 10 MINUTES PREPARATION • 30 MINUTES COOKING

I like to sear the fish so it is crisp on the outside and still a little rare in the centre, as such, it is important to speak to your fishmonger and buy the freshest fish fillets possible, from a type of fish that does not need to be cooked through.

2 bunches asparagus, trimmed, halved

100 g podded fresh or frozen broad beans

6 slices pancetta

1 onion, thinly sliced

100 g walnuts

1 tablespoon ghee (see page 194)

4 kingfish fillets, skin on

100 g feta

1/4 cup (small handful) flat-leaf parsley, finely chopped

sea salt and freshly ground black pepper

extra virgin olive oil, for drizzling

micro-herbs (optional), to serve

HONEY-MUSTARD DRESSING

1 tablespoon white wine vinegar

100 ml extra virgin olive oil

1 teaspoon dijon mustard

2 tablespoons honey

Preheat the oven to 180°C (160°C fan-forced).

For the dressing, combine all the ingredients in a small bowl, stirring until emulsified. Set aside.

Place the asparagus in a shallow roasting tin and pour over enough boiling water to cover, then leave for 5 minutes. Add the broad beans and leave for 1 minute, then drain and set aside.

Heat a heavy-based frying pan over medium heat and cook the pancetta for 5 minutes or until crisp. Remove and drain on paper towel, then tear into bite-sized pieces.

Turn down the heat to low, add the onion and saute for 10 minutes, stirring continuously to avoid colouring. Remove and set aside.

Scatter the walnuts on a baking tray and roast in the oven 5 minutes or until golden brown. Set aside to cool, then cut in half.

Heat the ghee in the cleaned heavy-based frying pan over medium heat, then add the fish, skin-side down, and sear for 3–4 minutes or until the skin is crisp. Flip the fish and sear for a further 1 minute or until just cooked through. Cut into bite-sized pieces.

To serve, combine the asparagus, broad beans, pancetta, onion, walnuts, feta and parsley in a large bowl, then add the dressing and gently toss through. Season with salt and pepper to taste, drizzle with olive oil and divide among 4 plates, then top evenly with the fish. Scatter with micro-herbs, if using.

Snacks

We all experience that mid-morning or afternoon slump and often reach for
sugary foods to give us a boost. However, it's protein, not sugar, that will boost
your energy levels to get you through to lunch or dinner. If you want to go for
a sweet snack, then make sure you pair it with a protein source, such as yoghurt
or nuts. For those of us on the run, this could be as simple as reaching for some
sliced ham and cream cheese on crackers or a handful of nuts with a piece of fruit.

Mushroom rillettes

SERVES 4–6
5 MINUTES PREPARATION
10 MINUTES COOKING

What is great about this dish is that the flavour develops the longer you leave it, making it perfect to throw together on the weekend so you have it ready to serve in the fridge for when you want a light bite during the week.

2 tablespoons ghee (see page 194)
300 g mushrooms, trimmed, roughly chopped
sea salt and freshly ground black pepper
2 cloves garlic, finely chopped
1/4 cup (60 ml) dry sherry
1 tablespoon lemon juice, or to taste
1 teaspoon finely grated lemon zest
1/4 cup (75 g) mayonnaise (I use the Japanese brand Kewpie)
finely chopped chives and poppadums, to serve

Melt the ghee in a heavy-based frying pan over high heat. Add the mushrooms and sprinkle in some salt and pepper. Saute for 4 minutes or until the mushrooms are tender, then add the garlic. Add the sherry, lemon juice and lemon zest, then bring to a simmer. Cook for 5 minutes or until most of the liquid has evaporated. Set aside to cool.

Transfer to a bowl. Add the mayonnaise and chives and season to taste, then add additional lemon juice if needed. Mix well and serve with crisp poppadums.

Transfer any leftovers to an airtight container, then refrigerate overnight to allow the flavours to develop.

Salmon and barramundi rillettes

SERVES 4
5 MINUTES PREPARATION
+ COOLING TIME
15 MINUTES COOKING

Although this is a quick and simple dish, it is a bit fancy, so keep it up your sleeve for when you want to impress.

1 × 150 g salmon fillet, skin off, pin-boned
100 g barramundi fillet
sea salt and freshly ground black pepper
1 tablespoon ghee (see page 194)
2 teaspoons chopped chives
2 teaspoons chopped dill
2 tablespoons mayonnaise (I use the Japanese brand Kewpie)
poppadums, caviar (optional) and fried lotus root (optional), to serve

Preheat the oven to 180°C (160°C fan-forced).

Place the salmon and barramundi on a baking tray, season with salt and pepper and top with the ghee. Cover with foil and bake for 10–12 minutes or until cooked through. Once cooled enough to handle, flake into small pieces.

Place the salmon, barramundi, chives, dill and mayonnaise in a bowl, season to taste and stir to combine. Serve with crisp poppadums, caviar and fried lotus root (if using).

Heirloom tomato and burrata salad

SERVES 4
10 MINUTES PREPARATION

Burrata is a fresh Italian cheese made from mozzarella and cream. This simple but classic combination is sure to please.

400 g mixed heirloom tomatoes, cut into
   bite-size chunks
sea salt and freshly ground black pepper
$^1/_2$ cup (handful) basil, roughly torn
1 golden shallot, finely chopped
extra virgin olive oil, for drizzling
balsamic vinegar, for drizzling
1 burrata cheese, at room temperature

Arrange the tomatoes on a serving plate. Season liberally with salt and pepper and sprinkle with the basil and shallot, then add a drizzle of olive oil and balsamic vinegar. Place the burrata in the centre and serve.

Shredded lamb and beetroot chutney on crostini

SERVES 1
5 MINUTES PREPARATION

I'm a big fan of leftovers. When cooking a roast, I always make a little extra so I can raid the fridge to prepare quick snacks like this.

leftover Slow-roasted Lamb
   (see page 116), shredded, as needed
Crostini (see page 70), to serve
Beetroot Chutney (see page 183) and
   baby cress, to serve

Serve the shredded lamb on crostini, topped with beetroot chutney and baby cress.

Quail scotch eggs

SERVES 6 • 20 MINUTES PREPARATION • 10 MINUTES COOKING

If you don't own a deep fryer, it's a good idea to use a deep-frying thermometer to check the temperature of the oil. Otherwise, drop a little panko crumb into the hot oil; it should bubble around it when hot enough to deep-fry. If using chicken eggs, follow the same process, but boil the eggs for 4 minutes first.

ice cubes

12 quail eggs

30 g butter

3 golden shallots, finely chopped

300 g sausage mince (if you can't find sausage mince, then buy the same weight of sausages and remove the meat from the casings)

1 teaspoon chopped flat-leaf parsley

sea salt and freshly ground black pepper

vegetable oil, for deep-frying

$^{1}/_{3}$ cup (50 g) plain flour

2 eggs, lightly beaten

1 cup (70 g) panko crumbs (see page 195)

1 tablespoon sherry vinegar

50 ml extra virgin olive oil

$^{1}/_{4}$ cup (small handful) baby cress

3 teaspoons capers in brine, drained

finely chopped chives and dijon mustard, to serve

Prepare a bowl of cold water and ice and set aside. Bring a saucepan of water to the boil over high heat. Add the quail eggs and cook for 2 minutes 10 seconds. Immediately transfer to the ice bath and leave to cool. Peel and set aside.

Meanwhile, melt the butter in a heavy-based frying pan over medium heat. Add the shallot and cook for 6–8 minutes or until translucent. Transfer to a bowl, add the uncooked sausage meat and parsley and season with salt and pepper, then stir to mix and set aside.

Heat oil for deep frying in a deep fryer or heavy-based saucepan to 180°C.

Place the flour, egg and panko crumbs in 3 separate bowls and season the flour with salt and pepper. Take each peeled quail egg, coat with flour, then press the sausage meat mixture around it to a thickness of about 1 cm. Dust evenly in flour again, then coat with egg and finally panko crumbs, gently pressing them on.

Carefully place each coated egg in the deep fryer and cook for 3 minutes or until golden. Carefully remove with a slotted spoon and drain on paper towel.

Mix the sherry vinegar and olive oil in a small bowl, then use to dress the baby cress.

To serve, season the scotch eggs with salt and pepper and serve with the baby cress, capers, chives and mustard to the side.

Coriander and chive tofu balls with grated beetroot, apple, carrot, zucchini and alfalfa

SERVES 4 • 10 MINUTES PREPARATION • 5 MINUTES COOKING

These tofu balls make a really healthy dairy-free snack, especially when paired with this tasty and equally healthy grated raw salad.

150 g silken tofu
300 g firm tofu, grated
1 tablespoon Garam Masala (see page 180)
small handful chives, finely chopped
handful coriander leaves, finely chopped
sea salt and freshly ground black pepper
$^1/_2$ cup (100 g) rice flour
ghee (see page 194), for cooking
1 carrot, grated
1 zucchini (courgette), grated
1 beetroot, peeled, grated
1 green apple, grated
100 g alfalfa
Classic Vinaigrette (see page 184),
    as needed

Place the silken and firm tofu, garam masala, chives and coriander in a bowl and season with salt and pepper, then mix thoroughly. Roll into 2 cm-diameter balls and coat with rice flour, then flatten slightly.

Heat 1 teaspoon ghee in a large heavy-based frying pan over medium–high heat. Working in batches if necessary, sear the tofu balls for 2 minutes on each side or until lightly browned and slightly crisp, adding extra ghee to the pan as needed.

Place the carrot, zucchini, beetroot, apple and alfalfa in a bowl, add enough dressing to just coat and toss to combine.

Serve the warm tofu balls on a bed of salad.

Mains

For many people, the main meal is the main event of the day. Although I believe in starting the day with a big breakfast, there's no doubt that it's rewarding to really put some effort and creativity into preparing satisfying dishes for dinner or substantial lunches. And, of course, your efforts are repaid with delicious leftovers that can sustain you for snacks and lunches the next day.

Chargrilled marinated chicken with bok choy

SERVES 4 • 15 MINUTES PREPARATION + 2–3 HOURS MARINATING • 15 MINUTES COOKING

Warning, you may need a bib for this one! These sticky, caramelised thigh fillets really do taste as good as they look.

2 tablespoons peanut oil or
    ghee (see page 194)
2 cm piece ginger, finely grated
2 cloves garlic, thinly sliced
$^1/_4$ cup (60 ml) mirin (Japanese rice
    cooking wine)
$^1/_4$ cup (60 ml) soy sauce
6 chicken thigh fillets, trimmed
1 bunch baby bok choy, trimmed, quartered
    lengthways and well washed
1 bunch broccolini, trimmed and cut into
    5 cm lengths
1 bunch choy sum, trimmed and cut into
    5 cm lengths
$^1/_4$ cup (35 g) unsalted peanuts, toasted
thinly sliced small fresh red chilli (optional),
    to serve

Combine the oil or ghee, ginger, garlic, mirin and soy sauce in a bowl. Place the chicken in a shallow glass or ceramic dish, then pour over the marinade and leave to marinate for 2–3 hours in the fridge, if time permits.

Arrange the bok choy and broccolini in the base of a steamer basket and place the choy sum on top, then cover with the lid. Sit the steamer over a saucepan of boiling water and steam for 2–3 minutes or until the vegetables are wilted and just tender. Set aside.

Preheat a chargrill pan over medium–high heat. Drain off the chicken, reserving the excess marinade. Chargrill the chicken for 5–6 minutes on each side or until slightly charred, caramelised and cooked through. Transfer to a plate, then cover and leave to rest for 5 minutes. Add the reserved marinade to the pan and bring to a simmer, then add the steamed vegetables and stir over medium heat to warm through and soak up the flavours.

Divide the vegetables among 4 bowls or plates and top with the chicken. Sprinkle with the peanuts and chilli (if using), and serve.

Crispy oven-fried chicken with cauliflower and fennel cream and star anise-pickled grapes

SERVES 4 • 30 MINUTES PREPARATION + 30 MINUTES TENDERISING • 30 MINUTES COOKING

This is my healthy version of fried chicken. It's just as good, if not better, than the real thing, without the guilt.

500 g chicken thigh fillets, cut into
    2 cm-thick strips
200 ml buttermilk
2 cups (300 g) buckwheat flour
    (see page 194)
1 teaspoon onion powder
1 teaspoon garlic powder
1 tablespoon paprika
2 teaspoons ground cumin
$^1/_2$ teaspoon cayenne pepper
2 teaspoons sea salt
$^1/_2$ teaspoon freshly ground black pepper
2 tablespoons ghee (see page 194)
Star-anise Pickled Grapes (see page 185) and
    baby cress, to serve

CAULIFLOWER AND FENNEL CREAM

ghee, for cooking (see page 194)
1 small onion, finely diced
1 clove garlic, peeled
$^1/_2$ cauliflower (about 500 g), broken into
    small florets
1 baby fennel bulb, thinly sliced
300 ml milk
sea salt and freshly ground black pepper

Place the chicken in a bowl and pour over the buttermilk, then cover and refrigerate for at least 30 minutes to tenderise.

Preheat the oven to 180°C (160°C fan-forced).

Place the flour, onion and garlic powders, spices, salt and pepper in a large mixing bowl and stir (or use a large zip-lock bag). Remove the chicken from the buttermilk, shaking off any excess buttermilk. Add the chicken to the bowl or zip-lock bag and roll to coat in the flour mixture.

Place the ghee in a roasting tin, using baking paper to spread it across the base. Place the chicken strips in the tin, making sure they don't touch. Roast for 15 minutes, then turn the chicken and roast for 10 minutes or until cooked through. Remove from the oven and set aside on paper towel to drain. Serve these warm.

Meanwhile, for the cauliflower and fennel cream, heat a little ghee in a heavy-based saucepan over low heat, then cook the onion and garlic for 8–10 minutes or until tender. Add the cauliflower, cover with the milk and bring to the boil over medium heat, then reduce the heat to low. Cook for 10 minutes, then add the fennel and cook for another 2 minutes or until tender. Drain the cauliflower and fennel, reserving the milk. Using a hand-held blender, blend the vegetables, slowly adding enough of the milk to achieve the consistency of creamy mash; you may not need all the milk. Season with salt and pepper.

Create a bed of cauliflower and fennel cream on each plate, top with 4 chicken strips each and cover the chicken with several grapes, making sure you add a teaspoon of the pickle juice to give it a bit of dressing. Scatter with the cress and serve.

Roast chicken with honey and tamari-roasted carrots

SERVES 4 • 20 MINUTES PREPARATION • 1½ HOURS COOKING

I've paired a classic roast chook with my favourite way to prepare carrots.

4 carrots, thickly sliced

2 leeks, white part only, well washed, thickly sliced

1 × 1.5 kg chicken

40 g butter, melted

½ teaspoon sweet paprika

½ teaspoon ground coriander

½ teaspoon ground cumin

¼ teaspoon ground white pepper

sea salt

large handful thyme sprigs

½ lemon, quartered

½ pear

6 cloves garlic, bruised

HONEY AND TAMARI-ROASTED CARROTS

2 bunches baby (Dutch) or heirloom carrots, trimmed, scrubbed, patted dry

¼ cup (60 ml) olive oil

⅓ cup (115 g) honey

sea salt and freshly ground black pepper

2 tablespoons tamari (see page 195)

sesame seeds, shaved parmesan and purslane (optional), to serve

Preheat the oven to 180°C (160°C fan-forced).

Scatter the carrot and leek in a roasting tin, place the chicken on top and brush with the melted butter. Sprinkle with the paprika, coriander, cumin and pepper and season with salt.

Tear the thyme and place it in the cavity with the lemon, pear and garlic. Secure the cavity with a metal skewer, tuck in the wings and roast for 1¼–1½ hours or until the chicken is cooked through; when it is ready the juices will run clear when the thickest part of a thigh joint is pierced with a skewer. Cover loosely with foil, then set aside to rest for 10–15 minutes.

Meanwhile, increase the oven temperature to 250°C or the highest temperature.

For the roasted carrots, spread the carrots in a roasting pan large enough to hold them snugly in a single layer, then drizzle with the olive oil and half of the honey, season to taste and roast for 15–20 minutes or until the liquid bubbles and the carrots start to caramelise. Pour the tamari and remaining honey over, toss to coat and season to taste with pepper.

Carve the chicken and serve with the roasted carrots scattered with the sesame seeds, parmesan and purslane.

Slow-roasted turkey

SERVES 4–6 + LEFTOVERS • 10 MINUTES PREPARATION •
8–9 HOURS COOKING + 30 MINUTES RESTING

This allows for leftovers for delicious mid-week salads and sandwiches. You can add sprigs of any additional herbs you have on hand to the turkey cavity before popping it into the oven.

125 g butter, softened

¹/₄ cup (small handful) thyme, finely chopped

¹/₄ cup (small handful) flat-leaf parsley, finely chopped

1 teaspoon Garlic Paste (see page 180)

1 pasture-raised turkey (about 4.5 kg)

2 large onions, quartered

2 carrots, cut into 3 pieces

sea salt and freshly ground black pepper

2 large lemons, quartered

1 cup (250 ml) white wine

Preheat the oven to 140°C (120°C fan-forced).

Combine the butter, herbs and garlic in a small bowl. Rinse the turkey and pat dry with paper towel. Using your fingers, gently loosen the skin of the turkey breast from the flesh. Rub the herb butter between the skin and the breast, then place in a roasting tin, breast-side up, and add the onion and carrot. Season the turkey all over with salt and pepper and stuff the cavity with the lemon. Pour the wine into the tin.

Truss the turkey with kitchen string and cover with foil, then roast for 6 hours, basting with the pan juices every 2–3 hours. Remove the foil and increase the temperature to 190°C (170°C fan-forced), then continue to roast for another 1–2 hours or until the skin is a rich brown and the meat has reached an internal temperature of at least 85°C when a thigh joint is inserted with a meat thermometer.

Leave the turkey to rest, covered loosely with foil, for 30 minutes prior to carving.

Quinoa chicken biryani

SERVES 8 • 30 MINUTES PREPARATION + OVERNIGHT MARINATING •
1 HOUR 15 MINUTES COOKING

Instead of using rice, I use quinoa as the base here as a healthier alternative – NASA has even considered giving quinoa to their astronauts during journeys as it offers a source of essential amino acids not usually found in plant-based foods. The spicy and complex flavours of the chicken are best if there is time to marinate it overnight.

2 tablespoons sweet paprika
1 tablespoon coriander seeds
1 tablespoon cumin seeds
1 teaspoon black peppercorns
2 teaspoons ground turmeric
1/2 teaspoon chilli powder
3 cardamom pods
2 cloves, coarsely broken
1/2 cinnamon stick
1/2 teaspoon finely grated nutmeg
3 star anise
3 fresh bay leaves
3 cloves garlic, roughly chopped
2 teaspoons coarsely grated ginger
100 ml vegetable oil
1 red onion, thinly sliced
1/2 cup (handful) roughly chopped mint
1/2 cup (handful) roughly chopped coriander
1 long fresh green chilli, finely chopped
sea salt
400 g Homemade Yoghurt (see page 181)
  or natural Greek-style yoghurt
1 kg skinless chicken thighs on the bone
300 g quinoa (see page 195)
80 g butter, chopped
coriander leaves and lemon wedges, to serve

Dry-roast the spices and bay leaves in a small heavy-based frying pan over medium heat for 2–3 minutes or until fragrant and toasted. Finely grind in a spice grinder or with a mortar and pestle until a powder forms.

Pound the garlic and ginger with a mortar and pestle, adding some water to make sure it loosens into a smooth paste. Set aside.

Heat the oil in a heavy-based saucepan over medium heat, then add the onion and cook for 6–8 minutes or until golden, stirring occasionally. Transfer the onion to a large glass or ceramic bowl, then add the herbs, green chilli, spice mix and garlic and ginger paste, season with salt and mix to combine. Add the yoghurt and stir to mix well. Add the chicken thighs to the marinade, then toss to coat well, cover and refrigerate overnight to marinate.

Cook the quinoa in a heavy-based saucepan of lightly salted boiling water for 15 minutes or until soft, adding more water if required if it starts to dry out.

Meanwhile, spread the chicken and marinade evenly in a large heavy-based saucepan or flameproof casserole dish, top with the butter, cover with foil, then a lid and cook over low heat for 45 minutes–1 hour or until the chicken is cooked through. Remove the foil and lid and cook for another 10 minutes to reduce the liquid and use a fork to shred the meat from the bones. Remove from the heat, remove the chicken from the pan and discard the bones.

Combine the chicken and sauce with the quinoa, then scatter with coriander. Serve hot with lemon wedges to the side for squeezing.

Roasted duck ragu
with pappardelle

SERVES 4–6 • 30 MINUTES PREPARATION • 4 HOURS COOKING

You could serve this satisfying, rich ragu with your favourite dried pasta.

1 duck
olive oil, for cooking
sea salt and freshly ground black pepper
2 red onions, thinly sliced
4 cloves garlic, thinly sliced
2 sticks celery, finely chopped
300 ml red wine, such as Chianti
2 × 400 g tins chopped tomatoes
100 g raisins
2 sprigs rosemary, leaves picked
3 fresh bay leaves
extra virgin olive oil, for drizzling
400 g pappardelle
shaved parmesan and flat-leaf
    parsley leaves, to serve

Preheat the oven to 180°C (160°C fan-forced).

Wash the duck, inside and out, then pat dry with paper towel and rub all over with olive oil, salt and pepper. Place in a snug-fitting roasting tin and roast for 2 hours or until golden, crisp and cooked through. Transfer the duck to a chopping board, cover with foil and set aside, reserving the tray to use later.

Place the onion, garlic, celery and a splash of olive oil in a deep heavy-based frying pan over low–medium heat. Cook gently for 10–15 minutes or until softened and light golden.

Meanwhile, wearing rubber kitchen gloves, remove the duck skin and discard, then shred the meat off the bones, discarding the bones.

Pour most of the red wine into the pan and simmer for 10–15 minutes or until reduced by half, then stir in the duck meat. Add the remaining splash of wine to the reserved roasting tin, then place over medium heat and scrape the lovely, crispy bits from the base of the tin and add to the frying pan. Add the tomatoes and 2 tins of water, then stir in the raisins, rosemary and bay and bring to a simmer. Simmer over low heat for 1½ hours or until the sauce has reduced and thickened.

Cook the pappardelle in a large saucepan of salted boiling water following the packet instructions. Drain.

To serve, divide the pappardelle among 4 bowls and top with duck ragu, then finish with a sprinkle of parmesan, a few parsley leaves and a drizzle of olive oil.

Beef stroganoff

This was my first audition dish for the *MasterChef Australia* judges and is my version of a childhood favourite.

1 tablespoon sweet paprika
sea salt and freshly ground black pepper
500 g beef fillet steak, sliced into
    4 cm × 1 cm strips
ghee (see page 194), for cooking
1 red onion, finely chopped
400 g wild mushrooms, cleaned, torn
100 ml brandy
2 cups (500 ml) Beef Broth (see page 33)
$^1/_4$ cup (60 g) sour cream, as needed
julienned raw beetroot, julienned
    gherkins, chopped flat-leaf parsley
    and sour cream, to serve

BROWN RICE PILAF

ghee (see page 194), for cooking
$^1/_2$ onion, finely chopped
1 carrot, finely chopped
1 cup (200 g) brown rice
2 cups (500 ml) Beef Broth (see page 33)
1 sprig thyme
1 fresh bay leaf
200 g frozen peas

For the rice pilaf, heat a little ghee in a heavy-based saucepan over medium heat and cook the onion and carrot for 8–10 minutes or until soft and translucent. Add the rice and cook for 1 minute, stirring continuously, then add the beef broth, thyme and bay leaf and bring to the boil. Cover with the lid, reduce the heat to low and cook for 25 minutes or until all the stock is absorbed and the rice is tender; 5 minutes before it is ready, add the peas and stir, then cover and continue cooking.

Meanwhile, mix the paprika and salt and pepper to taste in a large bowl and toss the beef through to coat thoroughly. Heat a little ghee in a large heavy-based frying pan over medium heat and cook the beef, turning once, for 2–3 minutes or until browned but still pink inside; do not cook for long as you want the meat to be medium–rare. Transfer the beef to a bowl and set aside.

Add the onion to the pan and cook over low heat for 8–10 minutes or until soft and translucent. Increase the heat to medium and add the mushrooms, then saute for 2 minutes or until golden brown. Add the brandy and simmer until reduced by half, then add the beef broth and simmer for 10 minutes or until reduced by half. Return the beef to the pan and warm through, then add enough sour cream until the sauce is the colour of a cafe latte. Adjust the seasoning if needed.

Divide the pilaf among 4 bowls and top evenly with the beef stroganoff. Sprinkle with beetroot, gherkins and parsley and add a dollop sour cream, then serve.

Simple beef stew

This is such a simple, yet satisfying dish. The simmered bones provide a really flavourful sauce, full of richness, essential fats and minerals, and the slow cooking process makes the meat really succulent. I like to serve this with crusty bread.

700 g beef shin (osso buccho, ask your butcher to cut into pieces)
sea salt and freshly ground black pepper
2 tablespoons ghee (see page 194)
2 onions, roughly chopped
2 large carrots, chopped into 4 pieces
2 sticks celery, roughly chopped
2 cups (500 ml) red wine
300 ml water
1 tablespoon Garlic Paste (see page 180)
2 fresh bay leaves
1 sprig thyme
1 tablespoon tomato paste (puree)
1 celeriac, peeled, cut into large chunks
1 tablespoon wholegrain mustard
roughly chopped flat-leaf parsley and squeeze of lemon juice, to serve

Preheat the oven to 160°C (140°C fan-forced).

Season the beef with salt and pepper. Heat the ghee in a large flameproof casserole dish over high heat and, working in batches if necessary, sear the beef, turning, for 8 minutes to create a caramelised sear on all sides of the beef until it is sealed but not cooked through. Transfer to a bowl and set aside. Reduce the heat to medium and add the onion, then cook for 8 minutes or until translucent. Add the carrot and celery and cook for a further 2 minutes.

Increase the heat to high and pour in the red wine, then, using a wooden spoon, scrape all of the caramelised goodness from the bottom of the dish (this adds so much flavour). Return the beef to the casserole dish, then add the water, garlic paste, herbs, tomato puree and celeriac and return to the boil.

Cover with the lid, then transfer to the oven to cook for 3 hours or until the beef is tender and coming away from the bone, stirring occasionally; add extra water if necessary.

Stir in the mustard and season to taste. Remove and discard the bay and thyme before serving.

To serve, scatter with parsley and add a squeeze of lemon.

Butter chicken

A friend of mine in India showed me how to cook the most amazing butter chicken in the world and I also learnt a few secrets on how to perfect it. I've refined it a little and would you believe only 2 tablespoons of butter . . . what?! Yes, the creaminess comes from cashews and trust me, it is so delicious.

7 cardamom pods

4 cloves

1 stick cinnamon

3 onions: 2 roughly chopped, 1 finely chopped

2 tomatoes, quartered

8 cloves garlic, roughly chopped

3 teaspoons ground coriander

1 teaspoon chilli powder

1 teaspoon salt

$^1/_2$ long fresh red chilli, chopped

1 cup (150 g) cashews

$^1/_2$ cup (125 ml) milk

40 g butter

vegetable oil, for cooking

ghee (see page 194), for cooking

1 kg chicken thigh fillets

fresh Roti (see page 178), basmati
    rice and natural Greek-style yoghurt
    (optional), to serve

TOMATO AND CORIANDER SALAD
250 g mixed cherry tomatoes, halved

1 tablespoon white wine vinegar

sea salt and freshly ground black pepper

torn coriander leaves, to serve

Tie the whole spices in a piece of muslin with kitchen string and place in a large heavy-based saucepan. Add the roughly chopped onion, tomato, half of the garlic, the coriander, chilli powder, salt, chopped chilli, cashews, milk and half of the butter and cover with the lid. Cook over low–medium heat for 45 minutes or until the onion is soft and fragrant. Remove from the heat and discard the spice bag, then leave to cool slightly. Working in batches, if necessary, blend in a blender until smooth and creamy.

Return the tomato mixture to the pan, then cook over medium heat for a further 20 minutes.

Place a heavy-based saucepan over medium heat and add the remaining butter with a drizzle of vegetable oil to prevent burning. Cook the finely chopped onion for 5 minutes, add the remaining garlic and cook for another 2 minutes, then add to the tomato mixture in the pan.

Meanwhile, heat a chargrill pan over high heat and add the ghee, then cook the chicken for 5–6 minutes. Turn and cook for another 5–6 minutes or until cooked through. Cut into bite-sized pieces and add to the tomato mixture, then gently stir to combine.

For the tomato and coriander salad, place the tomato and vinegar in a bowl, then season with salt and pepper and toss to combine. Transfer to a serving plate and scatter with coriander.

To serve, divide the rice and butter chicken among plates or bowls, or transfer to serving plates or bowls for guests to help themselves at the table. Serve with roti and the tomato salad alongside, topped with a spoonful of yoghurt, if desired.

Vietnamese beef salad

SERVES 4 • 25 MINUTES PREPARATION + 15 MINUTES CHILLING • 15 MINUTES COOKING + 15 MINUTES RESTING

This delicious beef salad is fragrant with lemongrass and mint and the crispy vermicelli adds a welcome crunchy element.

1 × 500 g piece grass-fed beef eye fillet, trimmed of sinew

2 tablespoons fish sauce

1 stalk lemongrass, white part finely minced

1 tablespoon peanut oil

1 cup (large handful) mint leaves, torn

2 golden shallots, thinly sliced

1 carrot, julienned

1 cup (80 g) red cabbage, finely shredded

1 Lebanese (small) cucumber, shaved into ribbons

$^1/_4$ cup (35 g) roasted unsalted peanuts, coarsely chopped

1 long fresh red chilli, seeded, julienned

coriander leaves, for scattering

LEMONGRASS DRESSING

1 stalk lemongrass, white part finely diced

1 teaspoon Garlic Paste (see page 180)

1 golden shallot, roughly chopped

1 fresh red birds eye chilli, finely chopped

$1^1/_2$ tablespoons fish sauce

30 g chopped palm sugar or soft brown sugar

$^1/_4$ cup (60 ml) lime juice

CRISPY VERMICELLI

200 ml vegetable oil, for deep-frying

100 g vermicelli noodles

$^1/_2$ teaspoon chilli powder

Preheat the oven to 160°C (140°C fan-forced).

Rub the beef with the fish sauce and lemongrass. Heat a large heavy-based non-stick frying pan over high heat and add the peanut oil. Add the beef and cook on all sides for 40 seconds each. Transfer to a baking tray and roast in the oven for 7 minutes for medium–rare, or continue until cooked to your liking. Remove from the oven and leave to rest for 15 minutes, loosely covered with foil, then wrap tightly in plastic film and place in the fridge to chill.

For the dressing, place all the ingredients in a blender and blitz until smooth. Set aside.

For the crispy vermicelli, heat oil for deep-frying in a large heavy-based saucepan to 180°C on a kitchen thermometer and add the vermicelli; it will puff up very quickly. Remove and drain on paper towel, then toss with the chilli powder and set aside.

Using a sharp knife, slice the chilled beef into 2 mm-thick slices and remove all of the plastic film. Transfer to a large bowl and toss with the mint, shallot, carrot, cabbage, cucumber, peanuts and dressing.

To serve, spread out the salad on a platter or 4 plates and top with the crispy vermicelli, chilli and coriander.

Slow-cooked spiced chicken thighs

SERVES 8 • 10 MINUTES PREPARATION • 50 MINUTES COOKING

You've probably guessed by now that I'm all about the one-pot wonder. This is a great dish for entertaining, as the spiced yoghurt marinade fills the house with a beautiful aroma as it bubbles away.

8 chicken marylands

1 teaspoon ghee (see page 194),
   plus extra for brushing

2 teaspoons sea salt

4 long dried red chillies

2 tablespoons coriander seeds

6 cloves

2 teaspoons black peppercorns

2 black cardamom pods, cracked

1^1/$_2$ teaspoons cumin seeds

^{1}/$_2$ teaspoon turmeric powder

^{3}/$_4$ cup (210 g) Homemade Yoghurt (see page 181)
   or natural Greek-style yoghurt

2 onions, finely chopped

2 cm-piece ginger, finely grated

3 teaspoons Garlic Paste (see page 180)

3 fresh bay leaves

1 stick cinnamon

sea salt and freshly ground black pepper

coriander leaves and sliced chilli,
   to serve (optional)

Pat the chicken dry using paper towel. Rub the ghee and 1 teaspoon salt over the chicken, then set aside for 5 minutes.

Meanwhile, toast the whole spices in a small heavy-based frying pan over low heat for 1 minute or until aromatic. Tip the spices into a coffee grinder and coarsely grind (or use a mortar and pestle). Add the turmeric and remaining 1 teaspoon salt and mix well.

Add half of the spice mix to the yoghurt, stir to combine, then cover with plastic film and refrigerate until required.

Lay the chicken pieces on a chopping board in a single layer and thoroughly rub the remaining spice mixture all over them.

Heat a large heavy-based frying pan over high heat until smoking hot. Brush some ghee on the base of pan and add the chicken pieces. (You could use a chargrill pan for this step – the idea is to sear the flesh of the chicken, not cook it through.) Cook for 5 minutes on each side, then remove from the pan and set aside.

Reduce the heat to medium, add the onion, ginger and garlic and sweat for 8 minutes or until soft. Add the bay leaves, cinnamon stick and spiced yoghurt to the pan and stir to combine well. Cook for 2 minutes, stirring constantly to avoid curdling the yoghurt; you will see the yoghurt slowly release water.

Add the seared chicken pieces to the pan, then increase the heat to medium and cook the chicken for another 5 minutes. Season the chicken with salt and pepper, then reduce the heat to low and simmer for 25–30 minutes or until cooked through and tender. Remove from the heat and leave to sit, covered, for 10 minutes.

Transfer to a serving bowl or divide among plates, scatter with coriander and chilli (if using) and serve.

Roast rack of beef with garam masala sweet potato, peas and spinach

SERVES 6 • 20 MINUTES PREPARATION • 1 HOUR COOKING

This dish is so versatile – you could use a lamb rack instead of the beef for a quick week-night option. Simply sear the seasoned lamb rack in a hot pan on all sides and then finish in a 250°C oven for 6 minutes, leave to rest for 5 minutes, then serve.

1 teaspoon ground cumin

1 teaspoon ground coriander

1 teaspoon Garlic Paste (see page 180)

1 teaspoon Ginger Paste (see page 180)

1 × 6-bone rack of beef

sea salt and freshly ground black pepper

GARAM MASALA SWEET POTATO, PEAS AND SPINACH

450 g sweet potato, cut into 1 cm dice

500 g frozen peas

50 ml ghee (see page 194)

1 teaspoon brown mustard seeds

1 teaspoon Ginger Paste (see page 180)

1 red birds eye chilli, chopped

$\frac{1}{2}$ teaspoon ground cumin

1 teaspoon ground coriander

1 teaspoon ground turmeric

1 cup (large handful) baby spinach leaves

1 teaspoon Garam Masala (see page 188)

5 sprigs mint

Mix together the cumin, coriander, garlic and ginger to make a spice rub. Massage the spice rub into the beef and place on a tray in the refrigerator to marinate overnight, if time permits.

Preheat the oven to 250°C (230°C fan-forced).

Place the beef in a roasting tin, season with salt and pepper and roast for 1 hour (I like the beef to be slightly pink on the inside) or until cooked to your liking. Remove the beef from the oven, cover loosely with foil and leave to rest for 30 minutes.

Meanwhile, for the garam masala sweet potato, cook the sweet potato in a heavy-based saucepan of salted boiling water for 10–15 minutes or until just tender. Drain well. Blanch the peas in a pan of boiling water, then drain and set aside.

Melt the ghee in a heavy-based frying pan over medium heat and fry the mustard seeds until they start to pop. Add the ginger and chilli and cook for 1–2 minutes or until they just start to colour. Add the spices, stirring constantly to prevent burning. Add the sweet potato and toss to coat, then season well with salt and pepper. Add the spinach, peas and garam masala and heat through slightly.

Slice the beef and serve immediately with the spiced sweet potato mixture.

Slow-roasted lamb shoulder with roasted vegetables

SERVES 4–6 + LEFTOVERS • 20 MINUTES PREPARATION • 4½ HOURS COOKING

This show-stopper is great as a centrepiece for a shared table. Accompany it with a few of my salads (see pages 52–86) to create a real feast.

1 × 1.5 kg lamb shoulder
2 tablespoons ghee (see page 194)
1 cup (250 ml) red wine
2 cups (500 ml) Chicken Broth (see page 33)
250 g mini truss tomatoes

SPICE RUB
1 teaspoon sweet paprika
1 teaspoon coriander seeds, crushed
1 teaspoon fennel seeds, crushed
1 teaspoon sea salt

ROASTED VEGETABLES
1 head garlic, halved widthways
2 red onions, quartered
4 potatoes, quartered lengthways
4 zucchinis (courgettes), cut into
    2 cm lengths
1 eggplant (aubergine), cut into
    5 cm × 2 cm lengths
4 sprigs thyme
juice of 2 lemons
50 ml olive oil
1 cup (250 ml) water

Preheat the oven to 220°C (200°C fan-forced).

For the spice rub, combine all the ingredients.

Coat the lamb shoulder with the spice rub. Heat the ghee in a flameproof roasting tin over high heat and cook the lamb for 5 minutes or until browned, turning once.

Deglaze the tin with the wine and broth, then pour over the lamb. Roast the lamb for 20 minutes, cover tightly with foil, then reduce the oven temperature to 160°C (140°C fan-forced). Roast for another 3–4 hours or until tender, basting occasionally; add the tomatoes for the last 30 minutes of cooking.

Meanwhile, for the roasted vegetables, place the garlic, onion, potato, zucchini and eggplant in a bowl, then add thyme, lemon juice and olive oil and season with salt and pepper. Transfer to another roasting tin and pour the water over. Roast for the last 2 hours while the lamb shoulder is cooking.

To serve, slice or shred the lamb, then serve with the tomatoes and roasted vegetables on platters or plates. (Leftover roast lamb will keep in the fridge for up to 5 days.)

Lamb backstraps with sweet potato colcannon and kale chips

SERVES 4 • 10 MINUTES PREPARATION • 40 MINUTES COOKING

Colcannon is an Irish dish traditionally made with potato and cabbage. My sweet potato version is a healthier alternative, as the natural sugars in sweet potatoes are slow releasing, giving you more energy for longer – plus, the flavours are sensational.

4 × 200 g lamb backstraps

olive oil, for cooking

2 sprigs rosemary

1 teaspoon Garlic Paste (see page 180)

sea salt and freshly ground black pepper

SWEET POTATO COLCANNON

1 kg sweet potatoes, cut into 4 cm pieces

sea salt

200 ml milk

100 g butter, roughly chopped, plus extra melted butter, to serve

¼ bunch kale, leaves shredded

sea salt and freshly ground black pepper

KALE CHIPS

½ bunch kale

1 tablespoon grapeseed or coconut oil (see page 194)

1 teaspoon salt

1 teaspoon sweet paprika or chilli powder

For the sweet potato colcannon, place the sweet potato in a large heavy-based saucepan in a generous amount of salted water. Bring to the boil and cook over medium–high heat for 30–35 minutes until tender. Drain in a colander and set aside to dry for 2–3 minutes. Return to the pan and coarsely mash.

Preheat the oven to 150°C (130°C fan-forced).

Meanwhile, for the kale chips, strip the kale leaves from the stems and tear into bite-sized pieces. Put the kale, oil, salt and paprika or chilli powder into a bowl and mix to coat. Spread the kale over a baking tray, then bake for 10–15 minutes or until crisp. Set aside.

Heat the milk and butter in a small heavy-based saucepan over medium heat for 2–3 minutes or until hot and the butter has melted. Add to the mashed sweet potato, a little at a time, stirring to combine to a smooth consistency. Stir though the kale. Season to taste with salt and pepper, drizzle with extra melted butter and serve hot.

Meanwhile, rub the lamb with olive oil, rosemary and garlic and season with salt and pepper. Preheat a chargrill pan over high heat. Cook the lamb for 5 minutes on each side for medium–rare or until cooked to your liking. Leave to rest for 5 minutes.

Slice the lamb and serve with the hot colcannon and kale chips.

Punjabi lamb kheema
in iceberg cups

SERVES 4 • 25 MINUTES PREPARATION • 35 MINUTES COOKING

This dish is high up on my list of favourite dishes. It can be eaten as a starter or a main. The spiced lamb balanced with the yoghurt gives an unforgettable taste explosion and will make it one of your favourites, too.

2 tomatoes, scored

ice cubes

1 tablespoon ghee (see page 194)

2 cardamom pods, lightly crushed

4 black peppercorns, lightly crushed

1 red onion, finely diced

2 teaspoons ground coriander

1 teaspoon ground cumin

500 g lamb mince

2 cloves garlic, crushed

2 cm piece ginger, finely chopped

1 long fresh green chilli, finely chopped

1 teaspoon sea salt

1 teaspoon ground turmeric

1 teaspoon chilli powder (if you like it hot, make it a tablespoon)

$1/4$ cup (60 ml) water

$1/2$ cup (60 g) frozen peas

2 teaspoons Garam Masala (see page 188)

$1/4$ cup (3 tablespoons) chopped coriander

iceberg lettuce leaves, trimmed into cups

Homemade Yoghurt (see page 181) or natural Greek-style yoghurt and micro-herbs (optional), to serve

Place the tomatoes in a bowl of boiling water for 30 seconds or until the skins start to slightly peel. Immediately refresh in a bowl of ice-cold water and roughly peel off their skins. Chop the tomatoes and set aside.

Heat the ghee in a large heavy-based saucepan over medium heat for 30 seconds. Add the cardamom pods and peppercorns and cook for 1 minute, then turn the heat down to low. Add the onion and cook for 6 minutes or until translucent; add a dash of water to stop the onion burning, if necessary.

Heat a dry frying pan over medium heat, then dry-fry the coriander and cumin for 30 seconds or until aromatic. Add to the onion mixture and stir. Increase the heat to high, then add the lamb, garlic, ginger and chilli and stir well to combine. Cook the lamb, stirring, for 5 minutes or until browned. (The high heat evaporates the liquid, which stops the meat from stewing, allowing it to brown – hearing it sizzle is a good sign.)

Reduce the heat to low–medium and add the salt, turmeric, chilli powder, tomato and the water, then stir through. Simmer for 20 minutes or until the liquid has almost evaporated. Add the peas and garam masala and stir, then cook for another 2 minutes or until the peas are cooked. Add the coriander and mix through.

Serve in iceberg lettuce leaves, topped with a spoonful of yoghurt and scattered with micro-herbs, if using.

Parmesan-crumbed pork cutlets
with Italian coleslaw

SERVES 4 • 25 MINUTES PREPARATION • 22 MINUTES COOKING

The key to perfect pork is not to overcook it. Trust your instincts and allow the pork to rest, as this will finish the cooking process without drying it out.

4 pork cutlets (about 280 g each), trimmed,
   bones French-trimmed (cleaned)
160 g panko crumbs (see page 195)
20 g parmesan, finely grated
2 tablespoons flat-leaf parsley,
   finely chopped
finely grated zest of 1 lemon
sea salt and freshly ground black pepper
1 egg
seasoned plain flour, for dusting
1/2 cup (125 ml) vegetable oil
80 g unsalted butter, coarsely chopped
lemon wedges and dijon mustard, to serve

ITALIAN COLESLAW
175 g podded peas (about 500 g unpodded)
1/4 white cabbage (about 300 g),
   very thinly sliced with a mandoline
1 baby fennel bulb, thinly sliced
   with a mandoline
1/2 red onion, thinly sliced with a mandoline
3 radishes, thinly sliced with a mandoline
1/2 cup (handful) basil, roughly torn
1/2 cup (handful) mint, roughly torn
1/2 cup (handful) flat-leaf parsley, coarsely torn
1/4 cup (small handful) watercress sprigs
1 tablespoon salted capers, rinsed
20 g parmesan, finely grated
1/3 cup (80 ml) extra virgin olive oil
2 teaspoons chilli oil
2 tablespoons lemon juice
sea salt and freshly ground black pepper

Working with one cutlet at a time, place between 2 pieces of plastic film and flatten with a meat mallet until about 1 cm thick. Repeat with the remaining cutlets and set aside until required.

Combine the panko crumbs, parmesan, parsley and lemon zest in a bowl, season with salt and pepper to taste and stir to combine. Lightly whisk the egg in a bowl and set aside. Lightly dust the cutlets in seasoned flour and coat with egg wash, then the panko mixture, shaking off the excess in between. Place on a baking tray and refrigerate until required.

For the Italian coleslaw, blanch the peas in a saucepan of boiling salted water for 1–2 minutes or until tender, then refresh in cold water and drain. Place in a large bowl with the cabbage, fennel, onion, radish, herbs, watercress, capers and parmesan and toss to combine. Just before serving, add the oils and lemon juice, season to taste and toss lightly to combine.

Meanwhile, preheat the oven to 160°C (140°C fan-forced).

Heat half the vegetable oil in a large heavy-based frying pan over medium heat, then add half the butter and heat until foaming. Working in batches, cook the cutlets for 4–5 minutes on each side until golden and cooked through. Drain on paper towel, then transfer to a baking tray lined with paper towel and place in the oven to keep warm. Wipe the pan with paper towel and repeat with the remaining oil, butter and cutlets. Season to taste, then serve hot with the Italian coleslaw, lemon wedges and dijon mustard to the side.

Pork and green peppercorn curry with pickled shallot

SERVES 4 • 10 MINUTES PREPARATION • 3 HOURS COOKING

A simple dish and another one-pot wonder, with an outstanding flavour. You can serve this with steamed rice, if you like.

1 tablespoon ghee (see page 194)

1 onion, sliced

2 teaspoons Garlic Paste (see page 180)

2 teaspoons Ginger Paste (see page 180)

1 kg boneless pork shoulder, diced

1 fresh red birds eye chilli

1 stalk lemongrass, white part only,
   thinly sliced

2 tablespoons tamarind paste (see page 195)

2 sprigs curry leaves, stalks removed

1 tablespoon mirin (Japanese rice
   cooking wine) or apple cider
   vinegar (see page 194)

1¹/₂ tablespoons Garam Masala (see page 188)

2 teaspoons ground turmeric

1 teaspoon chilli powder

sea salt

1 tablespoon green peppercorns

1 eggplant (aubergine), cut into 2 cm pieces

milk or coconut milk, to taste (optional)

Pickled Shallot (see page 184), to serve

Heat the ghee in a large heavy-based saucepan over medium heat and cook the onion, garlic and ginger for 10 minutes or until soft. Increase the heat to high and add the pork, then cook, stirring, for 5 minutes to caramelise and seal the pork; make sure the heat is high enough that the meat seals and doesn't stew. Add the chilli, lemongrass, tamarind and curry leaves and stir to combine.

Add the mirin or vinegar, then stir and add the spices, salt to taste and enough water to just cover the meat. Add the peppercorns and stir all the ingredients thoroughly. Cover the pan with the lid and bring to the boil over high heat. Reduce the heat to low, then stir the mixture thoroughly again and cook, covered, for another 3 hours or until the pork is tender.

Add the eggplant to the curry and cook for a further 10 minutes or until tender. If the curry is too spicy, add milk or coconut milk (about 2 teaspoons) to give it a milder taste.

To serve, divide the curry among 4 bowls and place the pickled shallot on top, then serve.

Pork belly and kimchi stew
with cauliflower 'rice'

SERVES 4 • 30 MINUTES PREPARATION + 1 HOUR MARINATING •
50 MINUTES COOKING

While I like to make my own kimchi, I often don't have the time. Instead, I buy it from Korean or Japanese stores, where it can be found in a stunning number of variations.

¼ cup (60 ml) tamari (see page 195)
1 teaspoon sesame oil
1 tablespoon finely grated ginger
1 teaspoon honey
1 kg boneless pork belly, cut into 2.5 cm dice
2 tablespoons ghee (see page 194)
8 fresh shiitake mushrooms
3 teaspoons Garlic Paste (see page 180)
3 spring onions, thinly sliced on the diagonal, plus extra to serve
3 cups (750 ml) Chicken Broth (see page 33)
300 g kimchi, drained and coarsely chopped
½ teaspoon chilli powder
½ carrot, coarsely grated
sea salt and freshly ground black pepper

CAULIFLOWER 'RICE'
1 kg cauliflower, broken into small florets, stems coarsely chopped
2 tablespoons coconut oil (see page 194)
sea salt and freshly ground black pepper

Combine the tamari, sesame oil, ginger, honey and pork in a large bowl and toss to coat the meat. Cover with plastic film and marinate in the fridge for 1 hour.

Heat the ghee in a large heavy-based saucepan over medium–high heat. Add the drained pork belly, reserving the marinade, and brown for 5 minutes, turning occasionally. Add the mushrooms, garlic and spring onion and saute for 1–2 minutes or until softened. Add the reserved marinade and chicken broth to the pan, then add the kimchi and chilli powder and bring to the boil. Reduce the heat to low and simmer gently, covered, for 35–40 minutes or until the pork belly is tender. Add the carrot, stir to combine and season to taste with salt and pepper.

Meanwhile, for the cauliflower 'rice', pulse the cauliflower in a food processor until it resembles grains of rice, if you like (or leave it chunky, as I have done here). Heat the coconut oil in a heavy-based frying pan over medium heat, then add the cauliflower and stir occasionally for 4–6 minutes or until softened. Season to taste, then serve with the pork belly and kimchi stew, scattered with extra spring onion.

Pulled pork

Is there anything better than pork crackling?

1 × 3 kg pork shoulder, bone in

melted ghee (see page 194) or olive oil, for cooking

sea salt and freshly ground black pepper

2 heaped teaspoons smoked paprika, plus
  extra for sprinkling

Preheat the oven to 200°C (180°C fan-forced).

Using a sharp knife, score the pork skin 1 cm deep all over. Drizzle a little melted ghee or olive oil over the pork and season generously with salt, pepper and paprika. Rub all over the skin, then place the pork in a roasting tin on the middle of the oven and immediately turn the temperature down to 160°C (140° fan-forced).

Roast for 4 hours, basting occasionally with the pan juices, then reduce the oven temperature to 150°C (130°C fan-forced) and continue to cook for another 2 hours or until you can pull the meat apart easily from the bone.

Remove the crackling and put it to one side, then remove any fat from the pan. Pull all the pork meat apart, discarding any bones and fat as you go. Using 2 forks, pull the meat into bite-sized pieces. Cover with foil until needed, then serve warm. (Leftovers will keep for 1 week in the fridge.)

Crispy-skin salmon with curry sauce and coconut sambal

SERVES 4 • 10 MINUTES PREPARATION • 35 MINUTES COOKING

One of the best tips I've picked up in India is to toast the spices before adding other ingredients, as this awakens their flavour and aroma. You'll know they're toasted when you smell that beautiful scent.

2 tablespoons ghee (see page 194)

4 × 200 g salmon fillets, skin on

basmati rice, Coconut Sambal (see page 184) and lime wedges, to serve

CURRY SAUCE

1 tablespoon ghee (see page 194)

10 fresh curry leaves

5 cloves garlic, thinly sliced

4 golden shallots, thinly sliced

6 cardamom pods, cracked

1 teaspoon fennel seeds

1 teaspoon fenugreek

$^1/_4$ teaspoon chilli powder

1 stick cinnamon

$2^1/_2$ tablespoons Sri Lankan Curry Powder (see page 191)

1 tablespoon ground turmeric

1 litre Fish Broth (see page 34)

1 cup (250 ml) water

2 cups (500 ml) coconut cream

juice of 1 lime

sea salt and freshly ground black pepper

For the curry sauce, heat the ghee in a heavy-based saucepan over medium heat. Add the curry leaves and fry for 30 seconds or until crackling. Add the garlic, shallot and spices and cook, stirring occasionally, for 5–7 minutes or until the shallot is tender. Add the curry powder and turmeric and fry for 1 minute or until fragrant. Add the broth and water and bring to a simmer over medium heat, then simmer for 20 minutes or until reduced by half. Add the coconut cream and bring to the simmer, then simmer for 5 minutes to reduce until slightly thickened. Strain the sauce, discarding the solids, then cover to keep warm.

Meanwhile, heat half of the ghee in a large heavy-based frying pan over medium–high heat. Cook the salmon, skin-side down, for 3–4 minutes, then turn and cook for another 2–3 minutes or until slightly pink in the centre.

Add the lime juice to the curry sauce and season to taste with salt and pepper.

Divide the rice among 4 plates, top with a piece of salmon, spoon some sauce over, then top evenly with the coconut sambal and serve with lime wedges to the side.

Steamed ocean trout with brown rice, fennel and preserved lemon salad

SERVES 4–6 • 10 MINUTES PREPARATION • 30 MINUTES COOKING

The clever use of spices is a great way to transform fresh ocean trout fillets into a satisfying meal, especially when paired with this vibrant salad.

600 g ocean trout fillets, pin-boned, skin off

1 teaspoon fennel seeds, coarsely crushed

1 teaspoon black peppercorns, coarsely crushed

sea salt

$^{1}/_{2}$ teaspoon ground coriander

$^{1}/_{2}$ cup (125 ml) water

lemon wedges, to serve

BROWN RICE, FENNEL AND PRESERVED LEMON SALAD

200 g brown rice

450 ml Chicken Broth (see page 33)

4 spring onions, thinly sliced on the diagonal

1 bulb fennel, thinly sliced

250 g cherry tomatoes, halved

large handful of fresh herbs (including mint, parsley, chives), torn

$^{1}/_{2}$ preserved lemon, rind only, rinsed, finely diced

60 g slivered almonds, toasted

40 g sultanas

juice of 1 lemon

$^{1}/_{4}$ cup (60 ml) olive oil

sea salt and freshly ground black pepper

For the brown rice salad, place the rice and broth in a heavy-based saucepan and cook according to the packet instructions. Remove from the heat and spread on a baking tray to cool.

Transfer the rice to a bowl and add the spring onion, shaved fennel, tomato, herbs, preserved lemon, almonds, sultanas, lemon juice and olive oil and stir to combine. Set aside.

Preheat the oven to 180°C (160°C fan-forced).

Place the ocean trout in a roasting tin, then coat with the fennel seeds, pepper, salt and coriander. Add the water to the pan, then cover with foil. Roast the trout for 10 minutes or until almost cooked; I like mine a little pink in the centre. Flake into bite-sized pieces.

To serve, divide the salad among shallow bowls or plates, then top with the trout.

Scallop and fish pie with cauliflower crust

SERVES 8 • 20 MINUTES PREPARATION • 1 HOUR COOKING

One of my fondest memories from living in London is snuggling up in front of an open fire, eating a tasty pie. This fish pie is truly delicious, but if you want to amp it up for a dinner party just add a hint of blue cheese into the mix – the umami flavour gives it that extra punch. You could halve the ingredients to serve four, if you prefer.

400 g firm white fish fillets, such as blue-eye
    trevalla or snapper
400 g smoked fish, such as haddock
350 g scallops, roe on
1 onion, finely chopped
1 carrot, finely chopped
1 leek, white part only, well washed, sliced
2 fresh bay leaves
2 cups (500 ml) milk
100 g frozen peas
20 g butter
30 g plain flour
200 g grated cheddar
sea salt and freshly ground black pepper
handful flat-leaf parsley stems
    and leaves, finely chopped

CAULIFLOWER CRUST
500 g potatoes, peeled, roughly chopped
$^1/_2$ head cauliflower, roughly chopped
45 g butter, plus extra for dotting
$^1/_3$ cup (80 ml) milk, warmed
sea salt and freshly ground black pepper

Place all the fish, the scallops, onion, carrot, leek, bay leaves and milk in a large heavy-based saucepan. Bring to a simmer, then reduce the heat to low and simmer for 10–15 minutes. Using a slotted spoon, transfer the fish and vegetable mixture to a bowl and strain the milk into a jug. Discard the bay leaves.

Blanch the peas in a small saucepan of simmering water for 4 minutes, then drain and set aside.

Melt the butter in a clean small, heavy-based saucepan over medium heat, then add the flour and stir with a wooden spoon for 5–7 minutes or until well combined. Slowly add the strained hot milk, whisking continuously until all the milk is incorporated and you have a smooth, thick sauce (ensure you bring it just to the boil to cook out the flour). Continue to cook over low heat for 5 minutes. Add the cheese and stir until it melts into the sauce. Remove from the heat, season generously with salt and pepper, then add the parsley and stir to combine.

Carefully add the white sauce to the fish and scallop mixture, along with the peas. Spoon into eight 1 cup (250 ml) capacity ramekins or a 2 litre pie dish.

Preheat the oven to 180°C (160°C fan-forced).

For the cauliflower crust, place the potato in a saucepan of water and bring to the boil, then simmer for 15 minutes or until tender. Drain, transfer to a bowl and mash, then set aside. Bring a saucepan of water to the boil and blanch the cauliflower, then drain. Add the cauliflower, butter and milk to the mashed potato and season with salt and pepper. Cover the fish mixture with the cauliflower mixture, using a fork to smooth the surface. Dot with extra butter and bake for 30–40 minutes or until the top is golden brown and the sauce is beginning to bubble up around the sides. Serve hot.

Crispy-skin fish with kale risotto and gremolata

The perfect weeknight meal – nutritious, filling and easy to digest.

1 tablespoon ghee (see page 194)
4 × 200 g firm white fish fillets, such as
    snapper, skin-on, pin-boned
sea salt and freshly ground black pepper
lemon juice, to serve

KALE RISOTTO
ghee (see page 194), for cooking
1 onion, finely chopped
1 teaspoon Garlic Paste (see page 180)
2 cups (2 large handfuls) kale, shredded
1 cup (200 g) brown rice
2 cups (500 ml) Chicken Broth
    (see page 33) or water
20 g butter
squeeze of lemon juice

GREMOLATA
finely grated zest of 1 lemon
2 tablespoons finely chopped flat-leaf parsley
1 teaspoon Garlic Paste (see page 180)
1 tablespoon extra virgin olive oil
sea salt and freshly ground black pepper

For the kale risotto, heat the ghee in a heavy-based saucepan over medium heat and cook the onion for 10 minutes or until soft. Add the garlic and kale and sweat for 3 minutes, stirring until wilted. And the brown rice and broth or water and bring to the boil, then reduce the heat to low, cover with the lid and cook for 20 minutes or until the rice is tender with a slight crunch.

For the gremolata, combine the lemon zest, parsley, garlic and olive oil in a small bowl and season well with salt and pepper. Set aside until ready to serve.

Meanwhile, heat a heavy-based frying pan over medium–high heat. Add the ghee, then season the fish well with salt and pepper and cook, skin-side down, for 4 minutes or until the skin is crispy. Flip the fish and cook for 1–2 minutes or until just opaque. Transfer to a plate and set aside to rest, uncovered.

Add the butter and a squeeze of lemon juice to the risotto and stir through until melted. Divide among 4 plates and place a piece of fish on top, skin-side up. Top with some of the gremolata and a drizzle of lemon juice and serve.

Hazelnut-crusted fish with cinnamon and thyme sweet potato fries

SERVES 4 • 10 MINUTES PREPARATION • 20 MINUTES COOKING

The hazelnut crumb does not quite brown as much as you would expect, so be careful not to overcook the fish.

1 cup (150 g) hazelnuts
coconut oil (see page 194), for cooking
1 teaspoon Garlic Paste (see page 180)
finely grated zest of 1 lemon
2 tablespoons chopped flat-leaf parsley
2 tablespoons extra virgin olive oil
freshly ground black pepper
4 × 250 g white fish fillets, such as blue-eye
    trevalla, kingfish or snapper, skin-off
$^3/_4$ teaspoon sea salt
lemon wedges, to serve

CINNAMON AND THYME
SWEET POTATO FRIES
400 g sweet potato, cut into 1 cm-thick chips
1 teaspoon ground cinnamon
$^1/_4$ cup (small handful) thyme leaves,
    finely chopped
coconut oil (see page 194), for cooking
sea salt and freshly ground black pepper

Preheat the oven to 200°C (180°C fan-forced).

Roast the hazelnuts on a baking tray for 5 minutes. Remove from the oven and place in a tea towel, then roll to remove the skins. Set aside.

Line 2 baking trays with baking paper and drizzle a little coconut oil over each one.

For the sweet potato fries, coat the sweet potato with the cinnamon, thyme, coconut oil and salt and pepper to taste. Place on one of the lined baking trays and roast for 15 minutes or until cooked through.

Meanwhile, combine the hazelnuts, garlic, lemon zest, parsley, olive oil and pepper in a food processor and process to form rough crumbs. Season the fish fillets with the salt and coat the top of each one evenly with a layer of the hazelnut mixture, using your fingers to press the crust firmly on. Place, skin-side down, on the second baking tray and bake for 12 minutes or until the crust is light golden and the fish is cooked through.

To serve, divide the fish and chips among 4 plates and serve with lemon wedges to the side.

Pan-fried barramundi with braised ham hock lentils and fennel salad

**SERVES 4 • 10 MINUTES PREPARATION •
30 MINUTES COOKING + 3 MINUTES RESTING**

Puy lentils are super-tasty and the best thing about them is that, unlike other legumes, they don't need soaking overnight.

4 fillets barramundi, skin on
sea salt

BRAISED HAM HOCK LENTILS

1 cup (200 g) puy lentils
1 tablespoon ghee (see page 194)
1 onion, finely diced
1 carrot, finely chopped
1 stick celery, finely chopped
$^1/_2$ bulb fennel (optional), finely chopped
100 g ham hock meat off the bone (or if can't
    find it use ham off-the-bone)
$^1/_2$ cup (125 ml) red wine
2 cups (500 ml) Chicken Broth
    (see page 33) or water
1 bay leaf
few springs of fresh thyme
sea salt and freshly ground black pepper

FENNEL SALAD
$^1/_2$ bulb of fennel, shaved with a mandoline
1 tablespoon white wine vinegar

For the braised lentils, cook the lentils in a saucepan of simmering water for 25 minutes or until just tender. Drain and set aside.

Meanwhile, heat the ghee in a heavy-based frying pan over medium heat. Add the onion, carrot, celery and fennel (if using) and sweat for 8–10 minutes or until translucent. Add the ham and cook for a further 4 minutes. Add the wine and bring to a simmer, then cook for 2 minutes or until reduced by half. Add the broth, bay leaf and thyme, then cover and simmer for 5 minutes over low heat. Add the lentils and stir to combine, then season to taste with salt and pepper.

For the fennel salad, place the shaved fennel in a bowl and add the vinegar, then set aside until ready to serve.

Heat a heavy-based frying pan over high heat. Score the barramundi skin at 1 cm intervals, season with sea salt and place in the pan, skin-side down. Cook for 2 minutes. Flip and cook for another 2 minutes or until just cooked through. Place on paper towel to drain for 3 minutes.

To serve, divide the lentils among 4 plates, then top each with a barramundi fillet and some of the fennel salad.

Ocean trout and smoked haddock fish cakes with homemade chilli jam

SERVES 4 • 25 MINUTES PREPARATION • 30 MINUTES COOKING

This dish is the perfect way to start an unforgettable food experience. The lightly smoked, aromatic fish is given a fluffy texture from the potato with a slight zucchini crunch. Serve it to your little ones with a dash of their favourite sauce or to your friends with a kick of my fresh chilli jam.

3 sweet potatoes (about 350 g), finely chopped
1 × 250 g ocean trout fillet, skin off, pin-boned
1 × 100 g smoked haddock fillet
sea salt and freshly ground black pepper
1 sprig thyme
1 stick celery, finely chopped
¹/₂ zucchini (courgette), coarsely grated
¹/₂ red onion, finely chopped
2 tablespoons finely chopped chives
¹/₃ cup (50 g) tapioca flour (see page 195)
1 tablespoon ghee
Homemade Chilli Jam (see page 183), to serve
fresh herbs, such as coriander or mint, to serve

Preheat the oven to 180°C (160°C fan-forced).

Place the sweet potato in a heavy-based saucepan over medium heat with enough cold water to cover. Bring to the boil, then reduce the heat to low and simmer for 15 minutes or until soft. Drain and place in a large mixing bowl.

Place the ocean trout and haddock on a baking tray lined with baking paper. Season with salt and pepper and add the thyme. Bake for 10–15 minutes or until just cooked through. Remove from the oven and flake the fish into bite-sized pieces, then add to the bowl of sweet potato.

Add the celery, zucchini, onion and chives to the bowl and mix together with your hands, then adjust the seasoning. Shape the mixture into about sixteen 5 cm-diameter balls, then flatten each until about 2 cm high.

Place the tapioca flour in a large bowl and use to lightly coat each fish cake, shaking off the excess.

Heat the ghee in a heavy-based non-stick frying pan over medium heat. If you can imagine the pan as a clock, add 6 of the fish cakes, starting at the 12 position, then 2, 4, 6, 8, and finally 10 position; this allows you to remember which cake you added to the pan first. Cook for 3 minutes or until the cakes are golden brown underneath, then flip the cake in the same clockwise order as before and cook for another 2 minutes or until the cakes are golden brown all over. Transfer to a plate lined with paper towel. Repeat until all the fish cakes have been cooked.

Serve with the chilli jam and fresh herbs.

Grilled prawns
with charred corn

SERVES 4 • 5 MINUTES PREPARATION + 20 MINUTES MARINATING •
10 MINUTES COOKING

This is one of my son Phoenix's favourite dishes. The sweetness of the corn with the tartness of the tamarind marinade is simply heavenly.

10 coriander roots, well washed

2 tablespoons tamarind paste (see page 195)

**2 long fresh green chillies, seeded,
roughly chopped**

2 teaspoons Garlic Paste (see page 180)

1 tablespoon lime juice

2 teaspoons maple syrup

sea salt and freshly ground black pepper

$^1/_3$ cup (80 ml) olive oil

**12 large raw tiger prawns, peeled,
cleaned, tails intact**

2 tablespoons grapeseed oil

1 teaspoon smoked paprika

2 corn cobs, kernels removed

**butter, lemon cheeks and micro-herbs
or cress, to serve**

SMOKED PAPRIKA MAYONNAISE

$^1/_2$ cup (150 g) good-quality mayonnaise

$^1/_2$ teaspoon smoked paprika

Place the coriander roots, tamarind, chilli, garlic, lime juice, maple syrup, ¼ teaspoon salt and some pepper in the small bowl of a food processor. Blitz and, with the machine still running, slowly add the olive oil to create a marinade.

Pour the marinade over the prawns, stir to coat and leave to marinate for 20 minutes.

For the mayonnaise, combine the ingredients in a small bowl. Set aside.

Combine the grapeseed oil and paprika to make a paste.

Heat a heavy-based frying pan over high heat until it starts to smoke. Immediately add the corn, and paprika paste and season with salt and pepper, then cook for 4–6 minutes or until slightly charred. Finish with a little dollop of butter and transfer to a bowl. Place the prawns in the pan and cook for 2 minutes, then turn and cook for another 1–2 minutes or until just cooked through.

To serve, divide the prawns among 4 plates and evenly spoon the corn mixture on top. Serve with lemon cheeks to the side, and scattered with herbs or cress, and the bowl of mayonnaise to the side.

Sichuan pepper and coriander mud crab with gai lan

SERVES 2 • 10 MINUTES PREPARATION • 20 MINUTES COOKING

You need to ensure that the crab is completely coated with the rice flour mixture as it soaks up any water, preventing the oil from spitting when the crab hits the hot pan.

1 × 1 kg raw mud crab

1 tablespoon Sichuan pepper, toasted

2 tablespoons coriander seeds, toasted

2 teaspoons sea salt

$^{1}/_{4}$ cup (50 g) rice flour

3 cups (750 ml) vegetable oil

3 spring onions, white and green parts
    thinly sliced

3 cm-piece ginger, peeled, cut into matchsticks

5 cloves garlic, chopped

1 bunch gai lan (Chinese broccoli), stems cut
    into 1 cm pieces and leaves shredded

2 tablespoons shao hsing rice wine

CHILLI OIL

100 ml grapeseed oil

1 tablespoon chilli powder

For the chilli oil, combine the oil and chilli powder in a small bowl. Set aside.

Remove the crab shell from the top of the body and clean, then reserve. Cut the crab body in half and remove and crack the legs and claws slightly. Set aside all the crab pieces.

Place the toasted Sichuan pepper, coriander seeds and salt in a mortar and crush with the pestle to form a medium–fine powder. Transfer to a large bowl, add the rice flour and stir to combine. Add the crab and toss to coat all over. Remove the crab from the seasoned flour, shaking to remove any excess and set aside.

Heat the oil in a large, deep heavy-based frying pan over high heat. Add the white part of the spring onion and the ginger and garlic to the pan and cook for 1 minute. Add the gai lan stems and cook for 2 minutes, then add the leaves and cook for another 2 minutes. Add the shao hsing and reduce by half. Working in batches, add the crab to the pan, carefully stirring the oil constantly, and cook for 3–5 minutes or until the crab legs are cooked, 5–7 minutes for the body and 7–10 minutes for the claws. Remove from the pan and set aside to drain on paper towel. Add the crab shell and cook for 1–2 minutes or until it turns bright orange. Remove from the pan and drain on paper towel.

To serve, transfer the crab mixture to a deep bowl, sprinkle with the green part of the spring onion and garnish with the crab shell, if desired. Drizzle with chilli oil, to taste.

Grilled salmon with romesco sauce and fennel and apple salad

SERVES 4 • 10 MINUTES PREPARATION • 5 MINUTES COOKING

I love making a big batch of romesco sauce and using it as a dip, in a sandwich or tossed with pasta – just about anything, really.

2 tablespoons ghee (see page 194)
4 × 200 g salmon fillets, skin on, pin-boned
sea salt and freshly ground black pepper
Romesco Sauce (see page 185), to serve

FENNEL AND APPLE SALAD
1 bulb fennel, thinly sliced with a mandoline
1 apple, peeled, cored, cut into matchsticks
$^1/_4$ cup (small handful) dill, finely chopped
juice of 1 lemon
sea salt and freshly ground black pepper

Heat the ghee in a large heavy-based frying pan over high heat. Season the salmon fillets with salt and pepper and place, skin-side down, in the pan, then cook for 3 minutes or until the skin is crisp. Flip and sear on the flesh side for a further 2–3 minutes or until the salmon has started to turn opaque for medium–rare. Transfer to a plate, cover with foil and set aside to rest.

For the salad, place the fennel, apple, dill and lemon juice in a bowl and season lightly with salt and pepper.

To serve, spoon a generous amount of romesco on 4 plates, add the fennel salad and top with the crispy-skin salmon.

Miso-glazed salmon with grilled asparagus and spring onions

SERVES 4 • 10 MINUTES PREPARATION • 10 MINUTES COOKING

There are no excuses for not making a quick weeknight meal with this super-simple and super-healthy recipe, as it only takes 20 minutes of your time.

$^1/_3$ cup (80 ml) mirin (Japanese rice cooking wine)

$^1/_4$ cup (70 g) white miso (shiro) paste (see page 195)

1 teaspoon honey

4 × 125 g salmon fillets, skin off, pin-boned

2 bunches asparagus, trimmed

1 bunch spring onions, trimmed

olive oil spray, for cooking

Combine the mirin, miso and honey in a shallow bowl. Add the salmon fillets and turn to coat.

Meanwhile, preheat the oven griller to medium heat and line the grill tray with foil. Spray the asparagus and spring onion lightly with cooking oil.

Drain the salmon fillets and arrange on the tray with the asparagus and spring onion. Grill for 5–10 minutes, turning once, until the salmon and vegetables are tender and the fish flakes easily.

To serve, divide the salmon and vegetables among 4 plates.

Tuna carpaccio with olive tapenade, watercress salad and mustard dressing

No heat, no loss of flavour, yet all the texture and all the nutrients – more to the point, this tastes so good that one plate is never enough. Perfect as a starter, this dish doubles as a healthy main for one.

1 × 200 g sashimi-grade tuna steak, thinly sliced
Olive Tapenade (see page 184), to serve
$^1/_2$ Lebanese (small) cucumber, finely diced
$^1/_2$ cup (handful) watercress sprigs
50 ml balsamic glaze
extra virgin olive oil, for drizzling
sea salt and freshly ground black pepper

Roll out a large sheet of plastic film on a large chopping board, place the tuna in a single layer on top, then cover with another sheet of plastic film, creating a tuna/plastic film 'sandwich'. Using the base of a frying pan, lightly tap the tuna to flatten without damaging the texture – it should be an even 1 mm thickness. Refrigerate to chill.

Just before serving, remove the tuna from the plastic film and place on a plate in a single layer.

Drop the olive tapenade in small amounts across the top. Scatter the cucumber and cress over. Drizzle the balsamic glaze and olive oil over the tuna. Season with salt and pepper, then serve.

Chilli-tomato mussel hotpot

SERVES 2
20 MINUTES PREPARATION
25 MINUTES COOKING

To prepare the mussels, soak them in a bowl of cold water for about 20 minutes. This allows the mussels to release any sand or dirt. To remove the beards, grasp each one between your thumb and forefinger and pull it downwards towards the hinged end of the mussel shell. Transfer the mussels to a fresh bowl of cold water using a slotted spoon, leaving the sand and dirt behind. Gently scrub each mussel under running water to remove any debris. I like to serve this with grilled bread (see picture opposite).

2 tablespoons ghee (see page 194)

1 onion, finely chopped

2 cloves garlic, crushed

2 small fresh red chillies, seeded, finely chopped

1 tablespoon tomato paste (puree)

$1/2$ cup (125 ml) dry white wine

500 g tomatoes, finely chopped

finely grated zest and juice of 1 lemon

sea salt and freshly ground black pepper

1.5 kg mussels, cleaned, bearded (see above)

micro-herbs or chopped flat-leaf parsley (optional) and grilled crusty bread, to serve

Heat the ghee in a large heavy-based saucepan with a tight-fitting lid over medium heat. Add the onion, garlic and chilli and cook for 8–10 minutes or until soft and translucent. Add the tomato paste and cook for a further 1 minute, then add the wine, tomato, lemon zest and juice and stir until well combined. Bring to the boil, then reduce the heat to medium. Simmer for 8–10 minutes or until thick. Season with salt and pepper. Increase the heat to high and add the mussels, then cover and cook for 3 minutes or until the mussel shells open.

Ladle the sauce and mussels into 4 bowls and sprinkle with parsley, then serve with crusty bread.

White-wine mussels

SERVES 2
20 MINUTES PREPARATION
10 MINUTES COOKING

This has to be one of my favourite weeknight meals – so simple to prepare and insanely delicious. The mussels cook a lot quicker than you may expect, so keep an eye on them, without opening the lid too many times as they cook in the steam.

1 tablespoon ghee (see page 194)

1 golden shallot or small onion, finely chopped

1 teaspoon Garlic Paste (see page 180)

100 ml white wine

500 g black mussels, cleaned, bearded (see opposite)

250 g cherry tomatoes

Heat the ghee in a heavy-based saucepan over low heat, then add the shallot and cook for 6 minutes without colouring. Add the garlic and cook for a further 2 minutes. Add the wine, then increase the heat to high and bring to the boil. Immediately add the mussels and cherry tomatoes, then cover with the lid and cook for 3 minutes or until the shells have just opened; take care not to overcook.

To serve, bring the pan to the table for everyone to help themselves, or spoon the mussel mixture into 4 bowls.

Buckwheat pasta with greens

SERVES 4 • 30 MINUTES PREPARATION + RESTING • 20 MINUTES COOKING

So simple but so good. Don't be overwhelmed by the amount of green vegetables in this dish, as they pack a flavour that will give you an epiphany – pasta dishes don't all need tomato, meat or seafood to be in your top ten. It's best to make the pasta dough the day before so it has time to rest in the fridge overnight.

salt

1 tablespoon extra virgin olive oil

$^{1}/_{2}$ onion, finely chopped

100 ml dry white wine

2 cloves garlic, crushed

$^{1}/_{4}$ head broccoli, cut into small florets

6 asparagus spears, finely chopped

1 cup (250 ml) Vegetable Stock (see page 35) or Chicken Broth (see page 33)

1 zucchini (courgette), coarsely grated

20 g butter

finely grated parmesan, basil leaves, lemon juice, finely chopped fresh red birds eye chilli (optional) and crusty bread, to serve

BUCKWHEAT PASTA

1 cup (150 g) buckwheat flour (see page 194)

1 cup (150 g) '00' plain flour

1 teaspoon sea salt

2 eggs, plus 2 egg yolks

$1^{1}/_{2}$ tablespoons squid ink (optional)

1–2 tablespoons olive oil

1–2 tablespoons water

For the pasta, combine both the flours and salt in a food processor. Whisk the eggs, egg yolks, squid ink and olive oil in a bowl. Add to the flour and pulse to blend. Add the water, a little at a time, pulsing until the mixture comes together to form a ball. Transfer to a lightly floured surface and knead until smooth. Wrap in plastic film and leave to rest in the fridge for at least 30 minutes, preferably overnight, if time permits.

Divide the dough into 6–8 pieces, then roll each one through a pasta machine, starting at the widest setting. Roll through and fold over 2 times (like a letter), then turn one-quarter and put through the machine. Repeat 3–4 times, dusting with buckwheat flour between each roll through to prevent sticking. Reduce the width of the rollers and roll through on each setting until you have reached the desired thickness – you don't want it too thin. Dust with more flour and leave to dry a little. Cut into 5 mm-thick strips and toss in a little flour so they don't stick.

Meanwhile, heat the olive oil in another heavy-based saucepan over medium heat. Add the onion and cook for 10 minutes or until translucent; add a dash of water to prevent it burning. Add the wine and reduce over medium heat for 2 minutes or until almost evaporated. Add the garlic, broccoli, asparagus and stock and cook for 2 minutes or until softened slightly through, then add the zucchini and cook for a further 5 minutes or until the liquid has evaporated. Add the butter.

Working in small batches, cook the pasta in a heavy-based saucepan of salted boiling water for 1–2 minutes or until al dente. Drain and set aside. Transfer the linguine to the greens and mix through.

Divide the linguine mixture among plates. Top with the parmesan, basil and a squeeze of lemon. Add chilli if you want an extra kick. Serve immediately with bread.

Drinks

Breakfast smoothie

SERVES 2
10 MINUTES PREPARATION

This is one of my 'on the go' breakfasts. The cinnamon-spiked banana flavour is paired with the sweetness of dates and slow burn of oats, so it is satisfying enough to take you through to lunch.

2 bananas
1 cup (90 g) rolled oats
1 cup (250 ml) milk
$^1/_2$ cup (140 g) Homemade Yoghurt (see page 181) or natural Greek-style yoghurt
1 teaspoon ground cinnamon
4 medjool dates, pitted
2 tablespoons LSA (linseed, sunflower, almond meal) (optional)
pinch salt
handful ice cubes
finely chopped unsalted pistachios, to serve

Place the bananas, oats, milk, yoghurt, cinnamon, dates, LSA (if using) and salt in high-powered blender with the ice and blend until smooth.

Divide between 2 glasses, scatter with pistachios and serve.

Pineapple and mint green smoothie

SERVES 2
5 MINUTES PREPARATION

A green smoothie doesn't need to be unappealing. I think it's great to kickstart your day with powerful ingredients, and what better way to do this than with a tasty green 'not gross' smoothie.

$^1/_2$ pineapple, peeled, cored, roughly chopped
$^1/_4$ cup (small handful) mint leaves
1 cup (large handful) baby spinach
2 cups (500 ml) coconut water or water
3 medjool dates, pitted
1 cup ice cubes
1 tablespoon desiccated coconut

Place the pineapple, mint, spinach, coconut water or water and dates in a high-powered blender with the ice. Blend until smooth.

To serve, pour into glasses, add the desiccated coconut and stir.

Choc-mint power smoothie

SERVES 2
5 MINUTES PREPARATION

1¹/₂ cups (375 ml) unsweetened coconut milk
  or Almond Milk (see page 179)
1 ripe banana
2 tablespoons unsweetened cocoa powder
1 tablespoon pure maple syrup
2 teaspoons peppermint extract (available
  from health food stores)
1 cup (large handful) baby spinach
handful fresh mint leaves
2 cups ice

Place the coconut or almond milk, banana, cocoa, maple syrup, peppermint, spinach and mint in a high-powered blender and blend on high for 45 seconds or until smooth. Add the ice. Cover and blend on high for another 15–20 seconds.

To serve, pour into 2 glasses. Serve immediately.

Revitalising green smoothie

SERVES 2
5 MINUTES PREPARATION

---

juice of 1 orange
1 cup (250 ml) coconut water
2 small frozen bananas, peeled, cut into chunks
¹/₂ large ripe avocado
1 teaspoon ground cinnamon
1 cm-long piece ginger, peeled
1 large handful spinach, silverbeet or kale

Place the orange juice, coconut water, banana, avocado, cinnamon, ginger and greens in a high-powered blender and blend on high until smooth. (If you do not have a high-speed blender just add more coconut water until it has blended.)

To serve, pour into 2 glasses. Serve immediately.

Mango lassi

SERVES 2–3
5 MINUTES PREPARATION + FREEZING TIME

---

3 frozen mango cheeks
1 cup (280 g) Homemade Yoghurt (see page 181)
  or natural Greek-style yoghurt
1 cup (250 ml) milk
¹/₂ teaspoon ground cardamom
¹/₂ teaspoon ground turmeric
small pinch salt
1 tablespoon honey
handful ice cubes

Place the mango, yoghurt, milk, spices, salt, honey and ice cubes in a high-powered blender. Blend on high until smooth.

To serve, pour into glasses and stir.

Pepper and spice hot chocolate

SERVES 6
2 MINUTES PREPARATION
5 MINUTES COOKING

2 cups (500 ml) milk

$^1/_2$ teaspoon ground cinnamon

$^1/_4$ teaspoon ground nutmeg

$^1/_4$ teaspoon chilli powder

$^1/_2$ cup (175 g) pure maple syrup, or to taste

$^1/_4$ cup (40 g) unsweetened cocoa powder

120 g bittersweet or semisweet chocolate, chopped

Whisk the milk, cinnamon, nutmeg and chilli powder in a large heavy-based saucepan over medium heat until the mixture begins to simmer. Reduce the heat to low–medium and add the maple syrup, cocoa powder and chocolate, then whisk until the chocolate is melted and the mixture is smooth.

To serve, pour the hot chocolate into 6 cups.

Indian tea

SERVES 4
2 MINUTES PREPARATION
20 MINUTES COOKING + 2 MINUTES STEEPING

1 litre water

1–2 thin slices fresh ginger

2–4 green cardamom pods, smashed

4 cloves

2 cm stick cinnamon

1 star anise

$^3/_4$ cup (180 ml) milk

$1^1/_2$ teaspoons loose black tea leaves

honey or pure maple syrup (optional), to taste

In a heavy-based saucepan, combine the water, ginger, spices and tea leaves. Bring to the boil over high heat, then reduce the heat to low and simmer for 10 minutes or until fragrant. Add the milk and simmer for another 10 minutes, then turn off the heat and leave to steep for 2 minutes; be careful as once the milk comes to a boil it may foam over, so be sure to turn the heat down if necessary.

To serve, pour into cups through a fine-mesh sieve. Discard the leaves and spices. Add maple syrup or honey, to taste, if desired.

Ginger tea a.k.a. the flu-buster

SERVES 1
2 MINUTES PREPARATION
5 MINUTES COOKING

1 cup (250 ml) water

2 cm-long piece ginger (or more to taste), peeled, finely grated

juice of $^1/_2$ lemon

1 teaspoon honey, or to taste

In a small heavy-based saucepan over medium heat, heat the water, ginger, lemon juice and honey until it reaches simmering point.

To serve, strain the tea into a mug.

Chai tea

SERVES 4
10 MINUTES PREPARATION
7 MINUTES COOKING

I usually drink this (see opposite) after I have a big meal. The subtle sweet flavour will complement your dessert and soothe your stomach at the same time. Perfect.

1 stick cinnamon

2 green cardamom pods

1.25 litres water

2 cloves

1 teaspoon black tea leaves (or 2 teabags)

2–4 cm piece ginger, grated

1 tablespoon honey, or to taste

$1^1/_2$ cups (375 ml) milk

grated dark chocolate or cocoa powder, to serve

Using a mortar and pestle, lightly crush the cinnamon and cardamom (or gently tap them with handle of a large knife or rolling pin).

Place the water, spices, tea, ginger and honey in a heavy-based saucepan over medium heat and bring to the boil, then reduce the heat to low. Simmer for at least 5 minutes – longer if you want a stronger flavour.

Add the milk, then heat for another 2 minutes; be careful as milk can easily boil over.

To serve, strain the tea into cups and top with grated dark chocolate or cocoa powder.

Desserts & sweets

If you are anything like me and have a massive sweet tooth, you need the option of having dessert. I've never been strong enough to ignore that craving for something sweet after dinner, so I was determined to provide some healthy options here.

Most of my recipes are naturally sweetened or lightly sweetened with fruits or maple syrup, so if you are used to sugary desserts, they may take a little while to get used to. However, trust me, they are all delicious and will satisfy that desire for a sweet finish to your meal.

Dark chocolate fudge with pistachios, basil and balsamic glaze

SERVES 10–12 • 5 MINUTES PREPARATION + 2 HOURS SETTING • 3 MINUTES COOKING

When I am entertaining, this is one of those dishes I can whip up in 5 minutes and leave to set in the fridge, to take the pressure off once my guests have arrived. Apart from the butter, I generally have all the ingredients in my pantry, but can mix things up to use whatever I have on hand. No baking, so it works a treat, when you want something sweet without turning the oven on.

200 g dark chocolate, finely chopped
1 × 395 g tin unsweetened condensed milk
50 g unsalted butter, chopped
$^1/_4$ cup (35 g) chopped unsalted pistachios
balsamic vinegar glaze, for drizzling
$^1/_4$ cup (small handful) small basil
   leaves, to serve
sea salt

Line a 20 cm × 20 cm slice tin with baking paper.

Place the chocolate in a microwave-safe bowl, then melt in the microwave for 30 seconds at a time, stirring as you go, until just melted; it will take 2–3 minutes. Fold through the condensed milk and butter until melted and well combined.

Pour half of the mixture into the tin and top evenly with half of the pistachios, then pour over the remaining mixture and top with the remaining pistachios, then drizzle with the balsamic glaze.

Cover with plastic film, being careful not to let it touch the fudge as it will stick, and leave to set in the fridge for a minimum of 2 hours or overnight. Remove from the tin and slice into bite-sized pieces. Store in an airtight container, layered between sheets of baking paper, for up to 1 week. Top with basil leaves and a pinch of sea salt immediately before serving.

Iced nougat

I am all for a balanced lifestyle and not restricting or eliminating the good things, and that includes dessert.

50 g caster sugar

70 g honey

1 tablespoon finely grated orange zest

50 g glucose

60 g egg whites

250 g thickened cream

2 tablespoons sultanas

30 g Craisins (dried cranberries)

25 g chopped pistachios

1 teaspoon rosewater

unsprayed rose petals, pomegranate seeds,
   Persian fairy floss, Turkish delight
   (optional), micro-herbs (optional),
   honey or pure maple syrup (optional)
   and rice paper (optional), to serve

Line a shallow 28 cm × 20 cm airtight container or baking tin with baking paper.

Place the caster sugar, honey, orange zest and glucose in a small, heavy-based saucepan. Bring to a gentle boil over medium heat until the mixture reaches 120°C on a sugar thermometer.

Meanwhile, using an electric mixer or hand-held electric beaters, whisk the egg whites until you see soft peaks. As the sugar mixture reaches 120°C, slowly pour it into the whisked egg whites to form a meringue. Continue to beat until the mixture has cooled to room temperature.

In a clean bowl, whip the cream until you see soft peaks. Fold the meringue, cream, sultanas, Craisins, pistachios and rosewater together. Transfer the mixture to the container or baking tin, cover with plastic film or the lid and place in the freezer to chill and firm. (It should set in 4 hours, but I like to leave it to chill overnight.)

Serve slices of the iced nougat with the rose petals, pomegranate seeds, fairy floss, Turkish delight, micro-herbs, honey or maple syrup and rice paper if using.

Cinnamon-spiced pumpkin custard

SERVES 6 • 10 MINUTES PREPARATION + 4 HOURS CHILLING TIME • 40 MINUTES COOKING

If you are a fan of pumpkin pie, then you will love this intriguing dessert.

400 g butternut pumpkin, peeled, seeded
³/₄ cup (180 ml) milk
140 ml pouring cream
3 large eggs, plus 3 egg yolks
¾ teaspoon ground cinnamon
¹/₂ teaspoon sea salt
¹/₄ cup (60 ml) pure maple syrup
1 tablespoon pure vanilla extract
finely grated nutmeg, to serve

CHANTILLY CREAM
300 ml pouring cream
1 teaspoon pure vanilla extract

Cook the pumpkin in a heavy-based saucepan of simmering water for 15 minutes or until tender. Drain and transfer to a blender, then blend to form a smooth puree.

Preheat the oven to 150°C (130°C fan-forced).

Place the pumpkin puree, milk, cream, eggs, yolks, cinnamon, salt, maple syrup and vanilla extract in a food processor or clean blender. Blend until smooth and well combined, then pour into 6 ramekins or heatproof jars.

Place the ramekins or jars in a deep baking dish. Fill the baking dish with enough hot water to come one-quarter of the way up the sides of the ramekins or jars.

Bake for 20–25 minutes or until the custards are just set; they will still have a slight wobble in the middle, which is perfect as they will set a little more as they cool. Remove the ramekins or jars from the water bath and refrigerate for 4 hours or until completely chilled.

Meanwhile, for the chantilly cream, whip the cream until soft peaks form and fold in the vanilla.

Just before serving, top the pumpkin custards with Chantilly cream and sprinkle with grated nutmeg.

Blackberry and coconut coulis with whipped coconut cream

I love this simple dessert. It is so quick to make, and has loads of tasty coconut flavours.

1× **400 ml tin full-fat organic coconut milk, refrigerated overnight**
1 **tablespoon pure maple syrup**
1 **teaspoon vanilla bean paste (optional)**
200 g blackberries, plus extra to serve
1 **teaspoon balsamic vinegar**
shaved coconut, crushed nuts, unsprayed rose petals or edible flowers (optional), small basil leaves and micro-herbs (optional), to serve

Carefully open the chilled tin of coconut milk, being careful to keep it level; there will be a firm, waxy, thick white layer of coconut cream on top. Scoop out the coconut cream into a large bowl or the bowl of an electric mixer; stop scooping when you reach the water in the bottom of the tin. Reserve the coconut water to blend with the blackberries.

Using hand-held electric beaters or the mixer on high speed, whip the coconut cream for 3–5 minutes until it becomes fluffy and light, with soft peaks. Mix in the maple syrup and vanilla, if using.

Blend the blackberries, 50 ml reserved coconut water and balsamic and pour evenly into 4 bowls.

To serve, scatter with shaved coconut, crushed nuts, rose petals or flowers, if using, basil and micro-herbs, if using. Top with a dollop of the whipped coconut cream.

Lemongrass panna cotta with fruit syrup

SERVES 6 • 10 MINUTES PREPARATION + 15 MINUTES STANDING + 4 HOURS SETTING • 5 MINUTES COOKING

This refreshing yet creamy dessert is the perfect finish for a dinner party as you can make the panna cotta in advance, then simply plate them when your guests are ready.

6 g gold-strength gelatine sheets

1 vanilla pod, split and scraped

1 stick lemongrass, bruised

300 ml milk

300 ml pouring cream

100 g pure maple syrup

micro-mint (optional), to serve

FRUIT SYRUP

1 mango, peeled, seeded,
   cut into 1 cm dice

1 slice fresh pineapple,
   cut into 1 cm dice

2 passionfruit, pulp removed,
   seeds strained

1 tablespoon pure maple syrup

$^{1}/_{2}$ cup (125 ml) water

Place the gelatine sheets in a bowl of cold water and leave for 5 minutes to soften.

Meanwhile, place the vanilla seeds and pod, lemongrass, milk, cream and maple syrup in a small heavy-based saucepan and bring to the boil. Immediately remove from the heat and leave to infuse for 10 minutes.

Place the softened gelatine in a small heavy-based saucepan with $\frac{1}{2}$ cup (125 ml) of the infused milk and bring to the boil over medium heat to dissolve the gelatine. Add to the remaining milk mixture and stir, then strain through a fine-mesh sieve, discarding the solids, and divide evenly among 6 × 95 ml dariole moulds. Refrigerate for 4 hours or until set.

For the syrup, place the mango, pineapple, strained passionfruit pulp, maple syrup and water in a bowl and stir to combine.

To serve, carefully invert the set panna cottas from the moulds onto serving plates. Spoon some of the fruit around the panna cotta, then drizzle some of the syrup around the outside and sprinkle with micro-mint.

Little pavlovas with citrus curd, passionfruit and basil

SERVES 6 • 30 MINUTES PREPARATION + OVERNIGHT COOKING • 55 MINUTES COOKING

You will need to make the meringues the day before so they can cool in the turned off oven overnight. You can either leave them whole or break them up, as I have done here.

melted butter, for brushing

1¹/₂ tablespoons cornflour, plus extra for dusting

8 eggs, separated (reserve the yolks for
     the lemon curd), at room temperature

sea salt

pinch of cream of tartar

2 cups (440 g) raw caster sugar

1 teaspoon pure vanilla extract

2 teaspoons white vinegar

pinch ground cinnamon

cream whipped with a little vanilla extract,
     passionfruit, orange segments and baby
     basil leaves, to serve

CITRUS CURD

8 egg yolks (reserved from making
     the meringues)

1 cup (350 g) honey

finely grated zest of 1 orange

¹/₃ cup (80 ml) orange juice

¹/₃ cup (80 ml) lemon juice

Preheat the oven to 150°C (130°C fan-forced). Line a baking tray with baking paper, brush with melted butter and dust with extra cornflour, shaking off the excess.

Place the egg whites in a large bowl with a pinch of sea salt and the cream of tartar, then using hand-held electric beaters or an electric mixer, whisk the egg whites until soft peaks form. With the motor running, gradually add the sugar, a tablespoon at a time, continuing to whip until the sugar has dissolved before adding more; this can take up to 20 minutes. The meringue should be glossy and all the sugar should be dissolved and not grainy. Reduce the speed to low and whisk in the vanilla and vinegar, then add the sifted cornflour and cinnamon and mix through.

Spoon one-sixth of the meringue at a time onto the baking tray into rounds, using a spatula to create little peaks around the sides of each one. Place in the oven and immediately decrease the temperature to 120°C (100°C fan-forced), then bake for 45 minutes. The meringues should be slightly dry and crisp on the outside, however they will really firm up once they cool. Leave to cool in the turned-off oven with the door ajar overnight.

To make the citrus curd, place the egg yolks, honey, orange zest and citrus juices in a heatproof bowl. Bring a saucepan of water to the boil over medium heat, then place the bowl on top, making sure it doesn't touch the simmering water (this is called a bain marie). Stir the egg yolk mixture continuously with a wooden spoon for 5–7 minutes or until it thickens and coats the back of the spoon. Strain through a fine-mesh sieve into a bowl, cover closely with plastic film and refrigerate until cool.

To serve, break up each pavlova and top with citrus curd and a dollop of freshly whipped cream, then spoon on the passionfruit, top with orange and scatter with basil.

Tapioca pudding with spiced watermelon

SERVES 4 • 10 MINUTES PREPARATION + 2 HOURS SOAKING • 15 MINUTES COOKING

I've combined the delicious texture of tapioca pearls, long-forgotten since my childhood, with gently spiced watermelon cubes to create a balanced dish that can be enjoyed as a dessert or first thing in the morning to kick-start your day.

1 cup (200 g) tapioca pearls

1 × 400 g tin coconut cream

1 cup (250 ml) water, plus
   1 tablespoon extra

1 tablespoon honey

1 tablespoon sesame seeds

micro-mint (optional), to serve

SPICED WATERMELON

1 teaspoon ground turmeric

1 teaspoon ground chilli

1 teaspoon coriander seeds

500 g watermelon flesh,
   cut into 2 cm cubes

1 teaspoon cumin seeds

1 tablespoon honey

Place the tapioca in a large bowl and cover with cold water. Set aside for 2 hours to soak. Drain the tapioca in a fine-mesh sieve.

Combine the coconut cream, water and honey in a heavy-based saucepan. Cook over low heat, stirring, for 1 minute or until the mixture just comes to a simmer. Add the tapioca and gently stir to combine, then cook for 4 minutes. Set aside.

Dry toast the sesame seeds lightly in a small frying pan and set aside to cool.

For the spiced watermelon, pound the turmeric, chilli and coriander seeds with a mortar and pestle until the coriander is coarsely ground. Add 300 g of the watermelon and pound until pulpy. Set aside.

Heat a heavy-based saucepan over medium–high heat, then add the cumin seeds and stir for 1 minute or until fragrant and starting to pop. Add the watermelon pulp mixture and simmer for 4–5 minutes or until the mixture starts to thicken. Add the remaining 200 g watermelon, stir to coat well with the sauce and cook for 2–3 minutes or until just warmed through. Season to taste with honey and salt.

To serve, divide the tapioca among 4 serving glasses, top with the spiced watermelon mixture and scatter with sesame seeds and micro-mint, if using.

Coconut chia pudding

If you are lucky enough to have leftovers of this luscious, creamy dessert, they can double as an easy, beautiful breakfast the next day.

$^1/_2$ **cup (25 g) flaked coconut**

$^1/_2$ **cup (5 g) chia seeds (see page 194)**

1 cup (250 ml) coconut milk

1 cup (250 ml) coconut water

1 teaspoon pure vanilla extract

$^1/_4$ **teaspoon sea salt**

$^1/_4$ **cup (85 g) pure maple syrup,**
plus extra for drizzling

$^1/_2$ **cup (70 g) macadamias, lightly toasted**
and crushed

seasonal fruit, such as mixed berries,
pomegranate seeds, figs, grapes,
and sliced strawberries, micro-herbs
and edible flowers (optional), to serve

Place the coconut, chia seeds, coconut milk, coconut water, vanilla, maple syrup and salt in a bowl and mix until very well combined. Soak in the fridge for at least 2 hours.

To serve, divide among 4 bowls, drizzle with extra maple syrup, scatter with crushed macadamias and top with the fruit of your choice.

Oat cookies

Melt dark or raw milk chocolate in a small heavy-based saucepan and drizzle over the cookies for an extra treat. You can easily double the quantities in the ingredients list to make a double batch, as I've done here.

1 cup (90 g) rolled oats

$^1/_2$ cup (25 g) coconut flakes

pinch sea salt

$^1/_2$ cup (60 g) chopped walnuts

$^1/_4$ cup (35 g) Craisins (dried cranberries)

1 ripe banana, mashed

40 g butter, melted

1 teaspoon pure maple syrup

1 tablespoon sesame seeds

Preheat the oven to 180°C (160°C fan-forced) and line a baking tray with baking paper.

Place the oats, coconut, salt, walnuts, cranberries, banana, butter, maple syrup and sesame seeds in a bowl and mix to combine. Roll 2 tablespoons of the mixture for each cookie into a ball and place on the lined tray, leaving space between them to allow for spreading.

Bake for 20 minutes or until golden and dry. Set aside to cool on the tray for 5 minutes, then transfer to a wire rack and leave to cool completely.

Basics

I learnt these basic preparations from my French cooking studies at Le Cordon Bleu and my son, Phoenix's, grandma (Bibi), who is Indian. She has taught me traditional Indian techniques, such as making yoghurt and fresh flatbreads, as well as pickles and chutneys.

Flax bread

For a dairy-free version, replace the butter with the same weight of coconut oil or macadamia oil (see picture on page 176).

200 g ground almonds
60 g arrowroot
100 g linseed (flaxseed)
1¹/₂ teaspoons bicarbonate of soda
1 teaspoon salt
3 eggs
60 g butter, melted
2 teaspoons pure maple syrup
1 teaspoon lemon juice
¹/₃ cup (80 ml) water

Preheat the oven to 180°C (160°C fan-forced). Line a 21 cm × 11 cm loaf tin with baking paper.

Place the ground almonds, arrowroot, linseeds, bicarbonate of soda and salt in a large bowl, then stir to combine.

Whisk together the eggs, butter, maple syrup, lemon juice and the water in a bowl. Add to the dry ingredients and stir to combine.

Spoon the mixture into the lined tin and bake for 30–40 minutes or until a skewer inserted into the centre comes out clean. Cool in the tin on a wire rack for 5 minutes, then turn out onto the wire rack and set aside to cool completely.

This bread keeps for 2–3 days, however, it freezes really well – cut into slices and wrap individually in plastic film, then freeze for up to 1 month.

Roti

Roti is one of the first dishes Phoenix's grandma, Bibi, taught me how to make – it is now a staple in my diet.

3¹/₃ cups (500 g) wholemeal plain flour
   (atta), plus extra for dusting
¹/₂ teaspoon fine salt
220 ml water
butter, to serve

Mix the flour and salt in a large bowl and make a well in the centre. Pour in the water and knead to make a smooth dough. Cover with plastic film or a damp cloth and leave to rest for 20 minutes.

Preheat the oven to 200°C (180°C fan-forced). Place a baking tray inside to heat.

Divide the dough into 6 portions and shape them into smooth balls. Dust with flour and flatten each to a disc, then roll out until about 3 mm thick.

Place the dough on the hot baking tray and bake for 4 minutes or until cooked through and patched with brown.

Coat one side with a little butter and serve warm.

Almond milk

You could add a shot of coffee for breakfast or a tablespoon of cocoa for a nightcap; I sometimes add 1 teaspoon each of ground cinnamon, nutmeg and cardamom for a spiced milk.

½ **cup (80 g) raw almonds**
pinch sea salt
5 medjool dates, pitted
1 tablespoon coconut oil (see page 194)
½ **vanilla bean**
1 litre water

Soak the almonds in water for 30 minutes, then rinse and drain.

Place the almonds, salt, dates, coconut oil, vanilla pod and water in a high-powered blender and blend on high speed until thoroughly combined and smooth. Strain through a fine-mesh sieve into a jug or bottle.

Almond milk will keep for up to 3 days in the fridge.

Garlic paste

Ginger paste

These mixes can be bought ready-made, however, it is very quick and much cheaper to make your own.

120 g (about 30) cloves garlic, peeled, coarsely chopped
¼ cup (60 ml) water
2 tablespoons olive oil

Place all the ingredients in a food processor or blender and blend to a fine paste.

I like to spoon the paste into ice cube trays and freeze. Once frozen, you can pop them all out into a Ziploc bag or container to take up less space in the freezer. One cube is about 1 tablespoon.

120 g fresh ginger, peeled, coarsely chopped
¼ cup (60 ml) water
2 tablespoons olive oil

Place all the ingredients in a food processor or blender and blend to a fine paste.

I like to spoon the paste into ice cube trays and freeze. Once frozen you can pop them all out into a Ziploc bag or container to take up less space in the freezer. One cube is about 1 tablespoon.

Homemade yoghurt

MAKES ABOUT 2 KG
5 MINUTES PREPARATION + 10–12
HOURS STANDING + 3 HOURS CHILLING

My son Phoenix's *bibi* (grandma) hasn't bought yoghurt for over 20 years. She has always made her own and this is something I picked up from her. There is nothing more satisfying and nutritious than making your own yoghurt. I don't believe in using low-fat milk, instead I buy good-quality full cream milk and drink it for its benefits. You will need a 2.5 litre capacity glass container with a lid.

2 litres full-cream milk
¼ cup (70 g) natural whole-milk yoghurt

Heat the milk in a heavy-based saucepan over medium heat. Using a probe thermometer, bring the milk to 82°C. Remove from the heat and set aside to cool until the temperature drops to 45°C. Stir in the yoghurt, then pour the mixture into the glass container and place the lid on.

Wrap the container firmly in a blanket, then place in a warm corner and leave undisturbed overnight, approximately 10–12 hours. The longer fermentation will yield a more tart yoghurt. (I personally like my yoghurt slightly more tart.)

Chill the yoghurt thoroughly, at least 3 hours; the yoghurt will thicken as it cools.

Labneh

MAKES ABOUT 400 G
2 MINUTES PREPARATION +
OVERNIGHT DRAINING

---

400 grams Homemade Yoghurt (see opposite) or natural Greek-style yoghurt

Strain the yoghurt in a fine-mesh sieve over a bowl in the fridge overnight; the longer you leave it, the thicker the labneh will be.

Condiments & pickles

Homemade chilli jam

MAKES ABOUT 1 X 500 ML JAR
15 MINUTES PREPARATION
50 MINUTES COOKING

$^1/_2$ small red capsicum (pepper), seeded,
  roughly chopped
3 fresh red birds eye chillies, roughly chopped
1 small onion, roughly chopped
1 tablespoon sea salt
100 g soft brown sugar
2 cm piece ginger, peeled, finely chopped
4 cloves garlic, crushed
200 g tinned chopped tomatoes

Place all the ingredients in a blender or food
processor and blend to form a roughly chopped
paste. Transfer the paste to a large heavy-based
saucepan over medium heat and bring to
the boil. Reduce the heat to low and simmer for
45 minutes, stirring occasionally. Spoon the jam
into a sterilised jar and cool in the fridge. (Leftover
chilli jam can be stored in a sterilised jar in the
fridge for up to 1 week.)

Beetroot chutney

MAKES ABOUT 1 X 500 ML JAR
10 MINUTES PREPARATION
35 MINUTES COOKING

---

4 beetroot, peeled, grated
1 cup (250 ml) red wine vinegar
1 cup (250 ml) apple juice
1 fresh bay leaf
1 sprig thyme
1 teaspoon ground cumin
1 teaspoon ground coriander

Place all the ingredients in a heavy-based saucepan
and bring to a simmer. Cook over low heat for
30 minutes or until soft and slightly jammy and
reduced. Remove the bay leaf and thyme and leave
the chutney to cool to room temperature. (Leftover
chutney can be stored in a sterilised jar in the
fridge for up to 1 month.)

Pickled onion

SERVES 4
5 MINUTES PREPARATION +
10 MINUTES STANDING

Make this just before serving.

$^1/_4$ cup (60 ml) red wine vinegar
$^1/_2$ red onion, thinly sliced

Pour the red wine vinegar over the onion in
a small bowl or jar and set aside for 10 minutes
or until ready to use.

Classic vinaigrette

MAKES ABOUT ½ CUP (125 ML)
5 MINUTES PREPARATION

100 ml olive oil
$^1/_2$ teaspoon dijon mustard
25 ml aged red wine vinegar
sea salt and freshly ground black pepper

Whisk the olive oil, mustard and vinegar until emulsified to form a vinaigrette. Season with salt and pepper. (Leftover dressing can be stored in an airtight container in the fridge for up to 4 days and used to dress leafy salads.)

Pickled shallot

SERVES 4
5 MINUTES PREPARATION
+ 5 MINUTES STANDING

100 ml mirin (Japanese rice cooking wine)
    or apple cider vinegar (see page 194)
100 g honey
1 French shallot, thinly sliced lengthways

Place the vinegar and honey in a heavy-based saucepan and bring to the boil. Immediately pour over the sliced shallot in a heatproof bowl and leave to pickle until ready to serve (5 minutes minimum) or until needed.

Olive tapenade

MAKES ABOUT ¾ CUP (175 G)
5 MINUTES PREPARATION

65 g black olives, pitted
25 g capers in brine, drained
1–2 anchovy fillets
$^1/_4$ cup (small handful) flat-leaf parsley leaves
extra virgin olive oil, for drizzling

Place all the ingredients, except the olive oil, in a food processor and pulse until finely chopped. With the motor running, slowly drizzle in enough olive oil to make a smooth paste. Transfer to a bowl, cover and refrigerate to chill. (Leftover tapenade can be stored in a sterilised jar in the fridge for up to 1 week.)

Coconut sambal

SERVES 4
5 MINUTES PREPARATION

1 tablespoon desiccated coconut
3 teaspoons chilli powder
1 small red onion, very finely chopped
1 teaspoon black peppercorns, crushed
sea salt

Combine the ingredients in a bowl, stir and season to taste with salt. Serve immediately.

Romesco sauce

MAKES ABOUT ¾ CUP (175 G)
10 MINUTES PREPARATION
+ 10 MINUTES COOLING
15 MINUTES COOKING

---

4 red capsicums (peppers), ribs and
   seeds removed, cut into chunks
2 tomatoes, cut into wedges
50 ml extra virgin olive oil,
   plus extra for drizzling
sea salt and freshly ground black pepper
1 cup (160 g) raw almonds, soaked
2 tablespoons balsamic vinegar
1 teaspoon Garlic Paste (see page 180)
1 tablespoon chopped dill
1 tablespoon chopped flat-leaf parsley
1 tablespoon chopped chives

Preheat the oven to 250°C (230°C fan-forced).

Toss the capsicum and tomato with the olive oil,
season with salt and pepper and place on a baking
tray lined with foil. Roast for 5–7 minutes, then
toss and roast for another 5–7 minutes or until the
capsicum is well browned and the tomatoes are
soft. Set aside to cool for 10 minutes.

Place the capsicum mixture, almonds, vinegar,
garlic, herbs and a drizzle of olive oil in a food
processor and pulse until a thick paste forms.
Season with salt and pepper and transfer to an
airtight container. (Leftover sauce can be stored
in a sterilised jar in the fridge for up to 1 week.)

Star anise-pickled grapes

SERVES 4
5 MINUTES PREPARATION + 30–40
MINUTES REFRIGERATING
3 MINUTES COOKING

$^1/_4$ cup (60 ml) white wine vinegar
30 g caster sugar
1 teaspoon fennel seeds
1 star anise
sea salt and freshly ground black pepper
100 g mixed red and green seedless grapes,
   halved lengthways

Add the vinegar, sugar and spices to a small heavy-
based saucepan over medium heat. Stir until the
sugar dissolves, then season with salt and pepper
to taste. Place the grapes in a heatproof bowl,
then immediately pour over the liquid to cover.
Refrigerate for 30–40 minutes to pickle, then serve.

Spices & pastes

Chilli salt

MAKES ABOUT 2 TABLESPOONS
5 MINUTES PREPARATION

This is one of my favourite spice mixes. I add it to so many things, from scrambled eggs and pasta dishes to sweet potato wedges and even my chocolate ganache. I make this in small quantities when I want to use it as it loses its zing when stored.

1 tablespoon chilli flakes
2 teaspoons smoked paprika
1 tablespoon Himalayan rock salt

Using a mortar and pestle, grind all the ingredients.

Herb salt

MAKES ABOUT 1⅓ CUPS (165 G)
5 MINUTES PREPARATION

The next time you roast root vegetables or a leg of lamb, try sprinkling them with this first as it really adds an instant kick of flavour.

8 sage leaves
$1/_4$ cup (3 tablespoons) picked rosemary leaves
2 tablespoons thyme leaves
1 cup (300 g) Himalayan rock salt
1 tablespoon chilli flakes
1 teaspoon fennel seeds
$1/_4$ teaspoon freshly ground black pepper

Pulse the herbs in a small food processor until coarsely chopped. Add the salt and spices and pulse to blend. Transfer to a 1½ cup (375 ml-capacity) jar.

Stored in a sterilised jar at cool room temperature for up to 2 months.

Spiced almond salt

MAKES ABOUT 120 G
5 MINUTES PREPARATION

Similar to dukkah, this adds great texture to soups, purées and pasta dishes. It is great to throw together when you want to take something simple up a notch, such as a poached or pan-fried piece of fish, barbecued squid or a grain-based salad

100 g raw almonds, dry roasted
$1/_3$ cup (50 g) sesame seeds, lightly toasted
2 teaspoons ground turmeric
1 teaspoon cumin seeds, ground
1 teaspoon black peppercorns, ground
$1/_2$ teaspoon sea salt
$1/_2$ teaspoon ground cinnamon

Using a mortar and pestle, grind all the ingredients until well combined. Store in a sterilised jar for up to 1 week.

Garam masala

MAKES ABOUT 1 CUP (120 G)
5 MINUTES PREPARATION

I always have this in my pantry as it means I can whip up Garam masala sweet potato, peas and spinach (see page 115) and loads of other Indian-inspired dishes in a flash. I use it as the base for nearly all of my Indian curries, or even add a sprinkle just before serving. My version includes fresh ginger, which really adds a warmth and depth of flavour compared to ready-made packets from the supermarket.

1/2 cup (35 g) coriander seeds

1/4 cup (25 g) cumin seeds

6 cm-long stick cinnamon, broken into
    9 or 10 pieces

2 tablespoons cloves

10 big cardamom pods

2 tablespoons small cardamom pods

1 1/2 tablespoons black peppercorns

1 nutmeg

2 cm-long piece ginger, peeled,
    roughly chopped

10 bay leaves

Using a spice grinder (or coffee grinder), grind the spices, ginger and bay to a fine powder. Transfer to a sterilised jar.

Garam masala can be stored in a cool, dry place for up to 1 month.

Chilli mix

MAKES ABOUT 1½ CUPS (185 G)
5 MINUTES PREPARATION + COOLING
3 MINUTES COOKING

This versatile spice mix gets a real workout in my kitchen. Sometimes I use it to dust a whole snapper or salmon fillet before pan-frying or grilling; other times I sprinkle it over sweet potato pieces before roasting to create healthy wedges. When you add a little bit of oil, it turns into a great marinade for meat.

1 1/2 tablespoons fennel seeds

1 teaspoon cumin seeds

1 teaspoon black peppercorns

1 teaspoon coriander seeds

1/2 cup (110 g) packed soft dark brown sugar

1/4 cup (55 g) raw sugar

1/3 cup (75 g) fine salt

1/4 cup (3 tablespoons) paprika

2 tablespoons smoked paprika

1 tablespoon garlic powder

1 teaspoon dried oregano

1 teaspoon cayenne

Toast the fennel seeds, cumin seeds, peppercorns and coriander seeds in a dry heavy-based frying pan over medium heat for a few minutes, shaking the pan, until the spices release an aroma. Tip into a bowl and leave to cool.

Blitz the toasted spices in a blender to a rough powder. Combine with the sugars, salt, paprikas, garlic powder, oregano and cayenne and mix thoroughly. Transfer to an airtight container and store in a cool, dry place for up to 2 weeks.

Harissa

MAKES ABOUT ½ CUP (150 G)
15 MINUTES PREPARATION +
20 MINUTES SOAKING

I love this North African version of chilli sauce and love how it really livens up a dish. Rub it on meat before grilling or simply serve it in a bowl with veggies alongside for dipping.

16 dried red chillies, stems removed, seeded

½ teaspoon caraway seeds

¼ teaspoon coriander seeds

¼ teaspoon cumin seeds

1 tablespoon mint leaves

¼ cup (60 ml) extra virgin olive oil, plus extra as needed

1½ teaspoons sea salt

5 cloves garlic, peeled

juice of 1 lemon

Place the chillies in a heatproof bowl, cover with boiling water and leave to soak for 20 minutes or until softened.

Toast the spices in a dry heavy-based frying pan over medium heat, swirling the pan constantly, for 4 minutes or until very fragrant. Transfer to a spice grinder (or coffee grinder) with the mint and grind to a fine powder. Set aside.

Drain the chillies and transfer to the bowl of a food processor with the ground spices, olive oil, salt, garlic and lemon juice. Process, stopping occasionally to scrape down the side of the bowl, for 2 minutes or until the paste is very smooth.

Transfer to a sterilised 2 cup (500 ml-capacity) glass jar, then add enough extra olive oil until there is a 1 cm layer of oil above the harissa. Refrigerate, topping with more oil after each use.

Store harissa in a sterilised jar in the fridge for up to 3 weeks.

Turmeric mix

MAKES ABOUT ¾ CUP (225 G)
10 MINUTES PREPARATION

Yoghurt is commonly used in Indian and Middle Eastern recipes as a marinade, to not only add flavour but to also tenderise meat and seafood. Try rubbing it over chicken fillets or prawn skewers before barbecuing or use it to marinate butterflied spatchcock before roasting.

2 large handfuls flat-leaf parsley, chopped

½ cup (140 g) Homemade Yoghurt (see page 181) or natural Greek-style yoghurt

2 cloves garlic, coarsely chopped

1 teaspoon ground turmeric

1 teaspoon ground cumin

juice of 1 lemon

extra virgin olive oil, as needed

sea salt and freshly ground black pepper

Place the parsley, yoghurt, garlic, turmeric, cumin, lemon juice, a good glug of olive oil and salt and pepper to taste in a blender and blend until smooth. Transfer to a bowl, cover closely with plastic film and refrigerate until needed. Use on the day of making.

Dukkah

MAKES ABOUT 170 G
10 MINUTES PREPARATION

This Middle Eastern spiced nut and seed mix is terrific to have on hand to add crunch and flavour to salads and vegetable accompaniments – I also sprinkle it over avocado on toast (see page 27) for a satisfying brekky.

100 g hazelnuts, roasted, skins removed
$^1/_3$ cup (50 g) sesame seeds, lightly toasted
2 teaspoons ground turmeric
1 teaspoon ground cumin
1 teaspoon black peppercorns, ground
$^1/_2$ teaspoon sea salt
$^1/_2$ teaspoon ground cinnamon

Using a mortar and pestle, coarsely grind all the ingredients. Store in a sterilised jar for up to 1 week.

Spiced seed mix

MAKES ABOUT 200 G
10 MINUTES PREPARATION

I really like adding seeds to salads and vegetable dishes as they provide a contrasting crunchy texture. I find it is worth spending 10 minutes to make this to have in my pantry, so I can create interesting salads in a flash.

1 cup (140 g) pumpkin seed kernels (pepitas)
$^1/_4$ cup (35 g) sesame seeds
$^1/_4$ cup (35 g) sunflower seeds
2 teaspoons extra virgin olive oil
1 tablespoon chilli powder (this is a lot, so feel free to adjust to your taste)
2 teaspoons paprika
$^1/_2$ teaspoon ground cinnamon
1 teaspoon Himalayan rock salt
1 teaspoon caster sugar

Place the pumpkin seeds, sesame seeds and sunflower seeds in a large cast-iron frying pan over medium heat. Stir frequently, for 3–5 minutes or until the seeds make a crackling noise; some will even pop. Remove the pan from the heat and stir in the olive oil, chilli powder, paprika, cinnamon, salt and sugar.

Leave to cool, then serve.

Sri Lankan curry powder

MAKES ABOUT ½ CUP (60 G) • 5 MINUTES PREPARATION • 35 MINUTES COOKING

This is a staple that I always have at the ready. Once you have made your own curry powder you will never go back to the bought stuff. I have given the proportion of spices I like, but feel free to experiment to suit your own taste.

1 tablespoon ground coriander

2 teaspoons sweet paprika

2 teaspoons salt

1 teaspoon ground cumin

1 teaspoon ground turmeric

1 teaspoon chilli powder

$^1/_2$ teaspoon ground fennel

$^1/_4$ teaspoon fenugreek seeds

1 cinnamon stick

10 fresh curry leaves

Pound all the ingredients with a mortar and pestle to form a powder.

Store in a sterilised jar in a cool, dark place for up to 1 month.

Chai mix

MAKES ABOUT 1 TABLESPOON
2 MINUTES PREPARATION

If you're after a chai fix in a hurry this is great to whip up to add to a warm glass of milk or almond milk before bed. To mix things up, I also use a teaspoon in my oat cookies on page 174 or my pumpkin custard on page 162 instead of the cinnamon, as well as adding it to custards and ice creams.

1 teaspoon ground ginger
1 teaspoon cinnamon
$^1/_2$ teaspoon ground cardamom
$^1/_2$ teaspoon cloves
$^1/_4$ teaspoon ground star anise
1 teaspoon caster sugar

Just before using, combine the spices and sugar in a bowl.

Gingerbread mix

MAKES ABOUT 1½ TABLESPOONS
2 MINUTES PREPARATION

I am a huge fan of ginger and sometimes add a sprinkle of this to smoothies and lassis for a zingy ginger hit. My favourite way of using this is to add a spoonful to my morning porridge.

1 tablespoon ground ginger
2 teaspoons cinnamon

Just before using, combine the spices and sugar in a bowl.

Pantry Staples

Apple cider vinegar

A fermented vinegar that is usually raw and unprocessed. Choose a raw and unfiltered one that retains the 'mother', as this contains strands of proteins, enzymes and good bacteria.

Buckwheat

This gluten-free grain is high in magnesium and protein, and can be used instead of rice. The flour can be used in breads, pizza bases and cakes. Found in health food stores and some supermarkets.

Buckwheat /soba noodles and pasta

Traditionally used in soups and Japanese dishes, they are also good in salads. Although primarily made from buckwheat flour, if you follow a gluten-free diet be sure to check the ingredient list, as some are thickened with wheat, and therefore contain gluten. Buckwheat pasta is high in magnesium and protein.

Chia seeds

High in Omega-3 fatty acids, fibre and antioxidants, these seeds are gluten free and easily digestible; they make a great gelling agent or egg replacement. Sprinkle on salads or soak to make chia porridge or pudding.

Coconut oil

It has a higher smoking point than many other oils, making it suitable for frying without burning.

Freekeh

Low GI and high in fibre, freekeh is roasted green wheat. It's a great alternative to rice.

Ghee (clarified butter)

Ghee is butter that has been heated until the milk solids separate, traditionally used in Indian cooking. Good for baking, roasting and frying.

Maple syrup

Available in various grades, this is a naturally occurring sugar with all its minerals still intact. There are also imitation maple syrups out there, so check the label and make sure it doesn't say 'maple syrup flavour'.

Miso

Miso paste is a Japanese fermented and ground blend of salt, soybeans and either rice or barley. The white (shiro) miso is sweeter and can be used in dressings and sauces. The darker varieties are saltier and more robust and should be used for stews and braised dishes.

Panko crumbs

Japanese-style breadcrumbs used as a coating on deep-fried foods to give them a good crunch. Available n packets from larger supermarkets and Asian food stores.

Pomegranate molasses

Made by reducing pomegranate juice down to a thick, intensely flavoured syrup, it is used in both savoury and sweet Middle Eastern recipes to add a sticky, slightly sour note.

Puffed rice

Commonly used in breakfast cereal or snack foods, it is a popular addition to some Indian dishes.

Quinoa

This popular gluten-free grain alternative is high in protein, manganese, lysine and other vital minerals. Rinse well in cold water before cooking to remove the wax-like coating saponin, which can leave a bitter taste and inhibit digestion. Use as a grain substitute in salads and breakfast dishes such as porridge or muesli.

Ras el hanout

This spice blend originated in North Africa and features heavily in Moroccan cooking. It can contain anywhere between 10 and 100 different spices, but typically contains cardamom, clove, cinnamon, coriander, cumin, paprika, turmeric and nutmeg.

Ricotta salata

A type of ricotta that has been pressed to remove the liquid, then salted and dried, resulting in a salty, semi-firm cheese that can be grated.

Seaweed (including nori sheets & wakame)

Edible seaweed can be purchased dried in larger supermarkets and Asian food stores. Fresh seaweed, such as wakame, can occasionally be purchased from select seafood suppliers.

Tamari

A Japanese gluten-free alternative to soy sauce. Mix equal amounts of tamari and tahini for a great alternative to satay sauce, or use on its own in stir-fries and marinades.

Tamarind paste

Made from soaking fibrous tamarind pods, then straining to create a tangy paste. It is used to add a sour note to many Indian and South-east Asian dishes, both savoury and sweet, such as Indian curries and chutneys in India, and Thai and Malaysian soups. It is also used in Mexican cooking.

Tapioca flour

This starch extract from the cassava root, also known as tapioca starch, is a gluten-free alternative to traditional wheat flour. It can be used instead of cornflour to thicken sauces and gravies, or to coat food to be fried.

Index

LANTERN

UK | USA | Canada | Ireland | Australia
India | New Zealand | South Africa | China

Penguin Books is part of the Penguin Random House group of companies
whose addresses can be found at global.penguinrandomhouse.com.

Penguin
Random House
Australia

First published by Penguin Australia Pty Ltd, 2016

1 3 5 7 9 10 8 6 4 2

Cover and text design by Holly McCauley © Penguin Australia Pty Ltd

Photography by John Laurie

Styling by Lee Blaylock

Typeset in Eames Century Modern by Post Pre-press Group, Brisbane, Queensland

Colour separation by Splitting Image Colour Studio, Clayton, Victoria

Printed and bound in China by RR Donnelley Asia

National Library of Australia
Cataloguing-in-Publication data:

Todd, Sarah, author.

The healthy model cookbook : 100 recipes to boost
your beauty and vitality / Sarah Todd.

ISBN: 9781921384363 (paperback)

Includes index.

Cooking. Nutrition. Diet. Cooking (Natural foods)

641.563

penguin.com.au/lantern